Praise for Unleash]

"Unleash Your Wings is a fantastic book. I literally couldn't put it down. The book helped me see how I, too, could create an extraordinary life. Raw, real and filled with simple, actionable steps, it's a book that changes lives."

Kerry Fisher,
Author, Life Coach, and Publisher

"The book was a total page turner. I read the whole thing in one sitting. Fran's story was so deeply moving and inspiring, that I felt all my limiting beliefs melt away through the wisdom in every single page. She is a true embodiment of resilience, faith, grit and pure, selfless love. I've read so many self help books, but this one touched my heart like no other. Absolutely brilliant read that you'll want to come back to again and again.

After reading this book, I learned that: 1: Faith can move mountains 2: The universe is always there to help you if you trust it and ask for support 3: Nothing in life stays bad forever. If you use it as a learning opportunity, it can propel you to greater heights than you ever imagined 4: It's never too late to start over 5: It's SO important to find your tribe and remove yourself from environments and people that don't serve you.

This book filled me with so much hope and positivity for my life. It also helped me shed some of the limiting beliefs I had as to what was possible for me. And it gave me the belief that no matter what raw materials are served to me, I can turn it into gold if I choose to."

Ramya Satheesh
Human Design Coach

UNLEASH
Your Wings

A Guide to Claim Your Unlimited Power and
Create the Life of Your Dreams

FRANCESCA FACIO

Library of Congress Cataloging-in-Publication Data
Names: Facio, Francesca, Author
Title: *UNLEASH YOUR WINGS*
LCCN 2024909593

ISBN 978-1-958165-29-4 (Hardback)
ISBN 978-1-958165-33-1 (Paperback)
ISBN 978-1-958165-34-8 (eBook)

Nonfiction, Mind, Body & Spirit, Self-Help, Personal Development

FOREWORD

*I*t is with great honor that I introduce you to the woman who has played such a significant role in my life as a teacher, a guide, a mentor, a leader, a colleague, a beautiful friend, sister, and confidante.

The way we met initially seven years ago was nothing short of spectacular and magic from the moment that I met Francesca Facio she was warm, loving openhearted, and had her arms spread open like a mama bear welcoming you into her own home.

Little did I know and realize she has now done this with every single woman she has met coached and inspired, which is now thousands and thousands of people from over 62 countries around the globe.

That is the magic and beauty of Francesca Facio, and it is now through these pages that you get to feel her essence and immerse yourself into the next chapter of your life.

Brace yourself because you will no longer be the same after this book.

You are in for the most beautiful expansive adventure with Francesca as your guide. Enjoy!

With her warm and generous heart, you feel it in her words as soon as you turn the pages of this book as she exudes it in her enthusiasm as a coach, sister, friend, healer, mother, and leader.

You are in for a treat with the amount of love and intention she has poured into each and every page, for you to step into your fullest transformation, spread your wings, and fully fly as you have always been meant for.

Dr. Neeta Bhushan,
5x Award Winning Author, That Sucked Now What, Top 50 Podcast Host The Brave Table, and Founder of the Highest Self Institute

PREFACE

This book was born after I almost lost my son in an accident when he was two. That fear, along with his autism diagnosis, made me extremely protective, and I tried to control everything to keep him safe.

When my daughter was born, I aimed to be the perfect mom and wife. I took on too many responsibilities, worked multiple jobs, and got into debt trying to provide the best for my family. I wanted to be a superwoman, but the pressure eventually caused me to break down. This breakdown helped me accept my imperfections and see life differently.

Afterward, I gave myself a personal honeymoon and freed myself from others' expectations. I found joy and discovered my purpose in coaching, helping thousands of people around the world. I've learned that everyone can create a life they love.

This book shares my stories and lessons as someone who let go of fear and control. It's about trusting that everything happens for a reason, finding beauty in life, and knowing you don't have to do everything alone.

Through these pages, you'll go on your own personal journey. You'll let go of what holds you back, reconnect with who you truly are, and learn to love yourself. You'll remember that you have the power to live an extraordinary life.

Welcome to your journey of rediscovery!

May your heart stay open to everything your soul desires.

CONTENTS

PART 1

WHAT MAKES YOU WHO YOU ARE

Most of us spend years carefully building the foundation of our lives.
Little by little incorporating what we are told is *the right way* to
live according to the rules of the society in which we are born.

Adding layers and layers of limiting rules and beliefs in an attempt
to fit into a fabricated *model of the world,* creating unrealistic
expectations for ourselves through the constant pursuit of perfection.

And we hold on to these self-imposed shackles with a
firm grip for as long as our soul can bear, holding tight,
looking for a sense of safety in what feels familiar.

But the day comes when something breaks, and we
finally throw away the mask that keeps our truth hidden
so we can see our true selves for the first time.

That is the day we wake up to a whole new world full of possibilities—
where we become creators of our own reality.

"Until you make the unconscious conscious, it will direct your life and you will call it fate."

– Carl Jung

CHAPTER 1

HOW YOU GET PROGRAMMED

When you are born onto this planet, you come with a clean slate. You are an unlimited powerful being who knows that you will be unconditionally loved and cared for. You know that everything you need will be provided for you, and all you have to do is ask. As a child, you tend to mirror the way that others perceive the world, observing and imitating the way others behave. This interaction gives you feedback and validation for how you should be, helping you refine your understanding of the world.

When you grow up and start incorporating language, everyone in your world gives you different commands on how your life should be lived. You start to get your first *labels* that help you make sense of the world, and this is where you start to associate meaning with everything that happens based on the labels that were handed to you. With this, you create your own mental models of what is right and what is wrong based on the manual of rules delivered by your parents and the society in which you grew up. And even though no one wants to cause you any harm, the people who raise you implant their own upbringing into you. This is how your personality is shaped and also how your limiting beliefs are born.

In the difficult time of adolescence, when you go from being a child who blindly believes what you are told, to figuring out the adult you want to become, you invest a lot of time and energy to try and redefine the system in which you were born. But external conditioning is a hard thing to change, so there comes a point in your life where you eventually end up adopting the beliefs of your surrounding culture because that is the only way you can "*fit*" *into your tribe.*

Let me tell you a little bit about my upbringing.

I was born in 1978 in Costa Rica. My childhood was beautiful and surrounded by love, but it was also guided by Latin American rules where there were certain scripts that you were expected to follow. Scripts that were very different for men and women, with a whole different set of rules according to your genitals. Parenthood was a clear example of this. Women were expected to be the primary caregivers of the family, putting anything else in their personal lives on the back burner to care for their children. That was what it meant to be a *good mom.* On the other hand, men were expected to financially support the family, but their lives didn't really change after a baby was born.

I became a mother at the tender age of 20. I was in my second year of college, living at my mom's house, with a stable job that I enjoyed and no worries beyond deciding where to hang out with friends after class or thinking about my next adventure. The future stretched out before me like an expansive realm of infinite possibilities.

At the time, I had a boyfriend in Nicaragua, and our relationship thrived on the excitement of seeing each other in small moments whenever we could. He traveled to Costa Rica, and I went to Nicaragua approximately every two weeks. For eight months, we focused on exploration, fun, and the pure joy of living in the moment. But after eight months of these back-and-forth trips, we realized that our long-distance relationship was no longer working, so I made one last trip to Nicaragua to say goodbye.

However, when I returned to Costa Rica, I found an unexpected companion. Three weeks after my return, when my period did not come as expected, I discovered that I was going to be a mother. The idea of becoming a mother so young not only scared me, but it felt like all the plans I had imagined for my future were shattered in front of me. I had to leave my life as I knew it and fully embrace my new role as a mom.

After considering all the options that were available to me, I realized I had only one choice that would allow me to live with myself, so I accepted the consequences of my decisions and embraced the fact that in the next nine months, I was going to be a mother. When I look at my children today, I can't imagine them prepared to embark on such a monumental responsibility at such a young age.

From that moment on, my life took a very different path than the one I had been living. For a moment, I felt like my life had suddenly stopped. I decided to get married because that was the *right* thing to do, and because my parents divorced when I was a child, so I wanted to give my baby a *fully functional family* experience.

I went to live in North Andover in Massachusetts, which is where my husband had the opportunity to work. I arrived when I was 19 years old in a strange and cold country where I couldn't work, so I became completely dependent on my husband for everything. For the first time in my life, I experienced what helplessness feels like. There was never enough food to eat, and I felt trapped in a relationship that became hostile due to the pressure of imposed responsibilities. My husband went from being a loving man with whom I shared occasional trips, to being an authoritarian man who felt frustrated by the abrupt end of his freedom.

We lived in a small apartment on the first floor where snow covered up to half the window of our living room. Extreme cold had never been part of my reality growing up in Costa Rica, and I felt like I could never get warm enough. Completely depending financially on my husband and with a very tight budget, I managed to get a couple of overalls and a sweater at The Salvation Army thrift store to survive the winter.

When my baby was born, he became a light in the rough environment I was in. I was living a life where I always felt like a bother to my husband, so I gave myself completely to motherhood and to giving all the love to my baby that I wasn't receiving for myself. I can remember the warmth I felt when I held him in my arms, the fullness he brought by just breathing, and the calmness he provided as I nursed him.

We named our son Eduardo. He was a bundle of joy, but his first months were very difficult. He slept very little, and I did not produce enough milk to meet his needs. My son's father never helped with anything, and he constantly criticized the terrible job I was doing as a mother and as a woman. Little by little, I became lost in a loop of responsibilities that I could not humanly sustain alone. The constant verbal attacks and the extreme loneliness with which I lived began to dampen my enthusiasm for living.

Thank God, I met two wonderful women from the condominium where I lived who *adopted* me and gave me support on the island of loneliness I was experiencing. They were the ones who helped me escape that life of misery. When I finally had nothing left to lose, my two friends helped me decide to end my abusive relationship, leave all my material things behind, and return to my country with my baby. I was terrified that someone would take Eduardo from me, but I knew I had to fight for my life and his. I got on a plane with my three-month-old baby, with the firm decision to protect the integrity of both our lives.

When I arrived in Costa Rica, my mother welcomed me with all the love that I had not received for more than a year. I arrived full of fears and insecurities, with scarcity and rejection permeating deep into my bones. When she took me to the supermarket and asked me to get whatever I wanted, I started bawling. I hadn't realized up to that point just how much scarcity I had lived with until I was presented with the gift of abundance again.

My ex-husband exploded in fury when I told him I wasn't coming back to the same loop of abuse. I told him that if he wanted to *fix* our relationship, he had to come to Costa Rica and agree to go to therapy. He didn't want to consider any other option than me coming back to the cold, so he started calling me in the middle of the night to vent his anger. The constant lack of sleep and fear created a paranoia of thinking that my baby could be taken away from me at any moment.

After a while and thanks to the love of my family, I began to rebuild my self-esteem and my courage. Little by little, I rebuilt myself to feel like a valuable person again. I also returned to finish my university studies, but I was no longer the same. While my classmates were busy with non-stop party plans, all my thoughts revolved around diapers and Barney songs. I felt out of place in a world where everyone lived a life very different from mine, so I stopped going out with my usual friends and isolated myself at home and school.

My young soul craved connection, but I had no idea how to balance motherhood and having a *normal life* that suited my age. Part of me wanted to go out and enjoy myself like everyone else, but another part of me knew that I had a big responsibility with my baby, and I needed to have all my energy for him. Sleepless nights, diapers, and breastfeeding completely took over my hours.

My mother always played a crucial role in helping me raise my son Eduardo. Without her support, I don't think I would have been able to cope with everything that was going on in my life. But a part of me wanted more. I still wanted to pursue the *ideal family* in some way, so after a year of returning to my country, I stopped complaining about my situation and started going out with other parents in children's playgroups. In doing so, I met the man who would later become my second husband.

Adrián was the father of an adorable 3-year-old girl named Camila. The fact that we both had small children helped us begin a relationship shaped by the circumstances of our lives. Our relationship was the beginning of a new stage in my young life as I was able to share many of my experiences as a mother with my partner. Between birthday parties and playgroups, we began to form a deeper sense of connection. I was no longer the young single mom who isolated herself at home. I now had a partner, so I could enjoy a little of the *normality* of raising young children as a couple. But no matter how much my life was *falling into place*, a part of me still felt sad about the things I was *missing* for a person my age, and I didn't know what to do with this feeling.

Journal Insight Questions

We all have a set of beliefs inherited by our family, our culture, our religion, and the people involved in our upbringing. These beliefs shape the way we understand our world, how we make decisions, and what we think is possible for us to create. Having an awareness of these beliefs is the first step to understanding ourselves better, and then being able to choose if they serve us or not.

- What are some of the beliefs that you hold on how you should live your life?
- Where did these beliefs come from? Your family? Your culture? Your religion?

"Life actually is this mystery and gift. And every moment of it can be full of real radical joy and wakefulness. And for some reason in our most difficult times, we have the best chance to wake up."

– Elizabeth Lesser

CHAPTER 2

THE UNIVERSAL "WAKE-UP CALL"

There comes a time when the Universe needs to shake you awake. This often happens when you cannot see beyond what is right in front of you and you need to change your current path so you can continue growing. The *wake-up call* is different for each person and can occur at any time in life. This is the moment when your current reality is shaken so that you can see a different perspective on life.

There are a couple of terms from Zen Buddhism that talk about the *wake-up call* in a way that really helped me understand how the Universe works: Kensho and Satori. Kensho and Satori moments are transformative experiences in which you gain a deeper understanding of your reality, your existence, or yourself. These experiences lead to a deep shift in your perspective, and each of them does it differently.

Kensho moments happen when you experience temporary pain or challenges. These are moments when life *hits* you. When you lose a loved one, when a relationship fails, when your business breaks, or any other moment that seriously sucks for you. These temporary experiences of pain allow you to steer the path of where your ego is taking you, to show you the path where your soul wants to go.

Satori moments are spurts of sudden enlightenment or awakening. They are these magical moments where you feel like you are on top of the world and you suddenly get an *"aha moment"* that makes everything clear. It is a profound spiritual experience that creates insight and helps you feel connected to everything. This is that feeling of Oneness that brings you clarity and peace.

Most of us would rather experience more Satori moments because Kensho moments are hard! Nobody wants to feel pain or struggle, but in the end, both are ways for you to get to the same place, which is **growth**. These moments are there for you to connect to why your soul chose to come to Earth and be able to honor that. As you continue working on your personal journey, Satori moments will become more common because you will be more receptive to what the Universe wants you to hear, and learn to navigate your life based on that.

As I was going through my personal *misery* story of how life had been so hard for me by becoming a teen mother, going through a divorce by the time I was 20, and how I was *missing out* on all the opportunities that were available for other people my age, I started to drown in my own victim story. My inner story didn't let me see beyond my pain to understand the greatness that was readily available to me. My soul was ready to move forward, but my ego was not allowing me to know exactly how.

The Kensho Moment that Changed My Life

On June 1, 2000, the Universe delivered my biggest *wake-up call*. The greatest Kensho moment of my life.

The day started like any other summer day in Costa Rica, with the sun shining brightly and my 2-and-a-half-year-old son, Eduardo, playing happily around the house. However, that day I was feeling sick, so my mom offered to take Edu to McDonald's so I could get some rest. She took him to play in the garden before leaving. Since we lived in a family condo, I always felt that Eduardo was safe.

Except for that day.

As I began to drift off to sleep on the living room couch, I suddenly heard a scream. It was that kind of scream that lets you know that something is wrong. Very, very wrong. I jumped from the sofa and ran toward the scream. My body tensed as the adrenaline rushed to every part of my body.

When I reached the source of the scream, my world came crashing down. My reality became blurry when I saw my baby boy lying on the ground next to my grandmother's car. He was not moving, and there were trickles of blood coming out of his nose and ears.

I know people were talking to me at the time, but I couldn't hear anyone. Their words were lost in the whirlwind of emotions and fear that consumed me. All my attention was on my son who was on the ground.

I took Eduardo into my arms and rushed him to the car. We needed to get to the hospital as quickly as possible; we knew that an ambulance would never get to where we lived in time. As I held my baby in my arms, the only thing I could say to him was, "Don't close your eyes, my love. Please stay with me." I repeated this over and over again.

As I caressed his little head, I could feel how the integrity of his skull was compromised, and it felt like it was jelly. I was terrified, but my sole purpose was to help him survive.

He can't die, not like this, I kept saying to myself.

When we arrived at the hospital, a group of emergency room doctors took my son from my arms and left me in a waiting room with my family for what felt like an eternity.

There was silence—the kind of silence capable of stopping time. I don't know how much time passed between when we took Eduardo to the hospital and the moment when the legion of doctors returned to the waiting room to give us news, but it felt like an eternity.

As I watched the large group of doctors enter the room with their faces full of worry and anguish, my heart skipped a beat. We were taken to a small conference room where I would receive the most devastating news of my life. They didn't know what to say or how to say it. It was too horrible for words, so what came out of one of the doctors' mouths was, "Have you considered organ donation?"

It was like a giant fist hit me directly in the chest and I couldn't breathe anymore. My entire being seemed to implode and I couldn't move. All I could think about was how surreal it was to hear the words *organ donation* in relation to my baby, who just a couple of hours earlier had been perfectly healthy playing in the yard.

My face must have hinted to the doctors that I needed more details. They explained that Eduardo only had a five percent chance of surviving. And if, by some miracle, he survived, he would likely be confined to a wheelchair for the rest of his life. The trauma to his brain was too great. The car had rolled on top of his little head, making it almost impossible for him to survive. I had to decide on organ donation quickly because none of us knew how much time he had left, and many other families of children were hoping to survive with such a donation.

I couldn't digest the news. I couldn't accept it. It was too horrible. This was my worst nightmare coming true. I got up from my chair and left the room, desperately searching for something that could return oxygen to my lungs. I stumbled upon a small chapel near the ICU of the Costa Rica Children's Hospital. I am not religious, but I am spiritual, and my soul guided me to that sacred space, as it does with so many who seek answers.

I sat on an empty bench and begged God to explain to me why my baby was on the brink of death. I begged him for a clear message, a way to make sense of this nightmare. I needed to understand why this was happening to my baby.

And then it happened.

At that moment, I received an image in my mind. It was a little boy playing with a train, which was Edu's favorite toy. He played with his train every day and loved it. Then one day, his train broke and the boy lost his cool. He started crying and called his father. His father entered the room and found the boy clinging to the broken train, crying inconsolably. The father calmly approached his son and asked him to give the train. After all, the father was an expert at fixing trains! The boy didn't know what to do, torn between wanting to give the train to his dad to fix it, and at the same time, not wanting to part with his beloved toy. The train was his.

The father gently explained, "I can't fix it if you hold on to it. You have to trust me and let it go."

At that moment, I realized that my baby wasn't really mine. He belonged to God and had been lent to me to care for him in this earthly experience as long as his soul needed me to do so. I left that chapel with the same feeling I had after giving birth—a feeling of emptiness in my belly, but it was also a profound feeling of peace. It was the same peace I felt when I was little in my dad's arms, trusting that everything was going to be taken care of by something much bigger than me.

As I walked down the hallway to return to the waiting room, I ran into my younger sister, Estefania. She was smiling, almost radiantly excited. I approached her gently, thinking she had no idea about the tragedy that had unfolded, ready to break the news. To my surprise, it was the other way around. She had just come from visiting my son in the ICU. The words she said sent a chill through my body:

"Did you see him? He is so beautiful! Eduardo is completely surrounded by angels!"

Then she sat me down and told me everything was going to be OK. The wise words that came out of her mouth were coming from somewhere outside of her. Something much bigger. It was as if she was channeling a divine message that was meant just for me to know that I was being held. And even though I cannot remember exactly what she said in that hour of conversation, her words spoke directly to my soul. It was as if she had sat with God Himself and He had spoken to her. My racing heart finally started to calm down and, somehow, I knew that Edu was going to be okay.

When I got to see Eduardo, his body was that of a 2-year-old baby, but his head seemed abnormally large, swollen from the trauma. The tubes coming out of his head to measure intracranial pressure created a blood-curdling image. I had to muster all my strength to see beyond the external signs of impending death and connect directly with his heart.

For the next two weeks, I spent every waking moment with Eduardo. I sent him love and healing light through meditation, inviting divine energy to heal every part of him. He had been placed in a medically induced coma to prevent further swelling of his brain, allowing his body to heal. He had his eyes closed and his body was inert. Yet somehow, I knew he was listening, receiving the love and healing energy from countless people around the world praying for him.

Amid the chaos of the Intensive Care Unit, I could hear the roar of multiple machines keeping other children alive, mixed with the painful screams of mothers whose children were losing their lives every day. Yet somehow, there was an inexplicable sense of peace surrounding Eduardo, as if all the healing energy and prayers were wrapping him in a protective cocoon.

Two weeks after the accident, Edu was taken out of a medically induced coma and moved to a private room. We all gathered around his bed, anxiously awaiting any sign of him waking up. You could feel the air in that room completely charged with expectation, all of us holding our breath to be prepared for any sign of life. Time moved extremely slowly like life had been put on pause. But then my baby moved.

Edu opened his eyes and began to moan. I urgently called the doctors who rushed to the room. Edu pushed them aside and pointed to my brother Fede, who was standing at the foot of his bed. My brother was eating some McDonald's fries and Edu pointed them out. This might seem like a simple thing to anyone, but for me, it was monumental. He had not lost his memory, and he remembered his favorite food—the fries he was going to get the day the accident happened.

A few days later, Edu was discharged from the hospital, and, to our surprise, he was still the same happy baby as always. All the dire consequences the doctors had warned us about now felt like distant threats. Eduardo retained all his memories from before the accident and could move freely as if nothing had ever happened to him.

About a month later, I took him back to the hospital for another CT scan. When I handed the first CT scan to the technician, he couldn't believe it belonged to the little human running energetically around the room. I had to call the neurosurgeon who saw Eduardo during his accident to confirm to the technician that the CT scan he had in his hands belonged to my son and had been performed less than a month prior.

"But doctor, this CT scan is of a deceased patient. There is no way someone could survive an injury like this," the technician exclaimed.

"I know," the doctor replied, "I didn't think miracles were possible either."

Although Eduardo's challenges were not over after this first miracle, today my son is a portrait of happiness and health. Not only did he complete college with two different degrees, but now he is following his passion of becoming a voice-over actor.

That experience marked my first deep awakening of the Universe. Of course, this nightmare was not something that I would have ever wanted, especially not for my baby boy, but that deep lesson that I learned after Eduardo's accident completely shifted my life. It was the first time in my 22 years that I truly understood that there was a reality much greater than the limited world I had known up to that point.

Journal Insight Questions

Your Kensho Moments:

- Have you ever experienced a Kensho moment? A moment where you felt like you had been punched in the gut with no control over the development of the situation? For example: a breakup, a loss, deep fear, and pain.
- Write this down.
- Allow yourself to feel your emotions for a couple of minutes.
- Then write something that you learned about life, something that changed within you as a result of this Kensho moment. Did you gain a different perspective on how you see life today because of what happened? Or did your understanding of life change? Did you change?
- Do this exercise with every Kensho moment you can remember. This will help you to see that your hardest moments brought you gifts.

Your Satori Moments:

- Make a list of all your Satori moments. The moments where you felt a surge of inspiration, awe, and enlightenment that helped you understand things from a higher perspective.
- Allow yourself to feel your emotions for a couple of minutes.
- Then reflect on what those moments taught you, and write it down.

"I'm firmly convinced that true beauty only springs from the acceptance of oneself, from an awareness of who we really are."

– Peter Lindbergh

CHAPTER 3

YOU ARE ONLY
HUMAN

I saw this video from Jay Shetty once where he explains in simple terms the way that human life works by comparing our life experiences with the beating of our hearts. When you see a flat line in an ECG machine, this means you are dead. And if you see the heart beating up and down, it means you are alive. Such a simple, yet profound fact.

Life moves like our human heartbeat; it is filled with ups and downs, moments that will uplift you, and moments where you will be thrown to the ground. And just like our heartbeat, these moments will come and go; they will move you up and down over and over again. We are meant to experience *everything* because this is how we get traction to keep moving forward.

Start by acknowledging you are *human*, and you are *alive*. Just by recognizing these two simple truths, you can start to let go of the false illusion of wanting a life without any events that will take you out of the sameness. Remember that nothing lasts forever, and you will deal with what comes when it comes. Just give yourself grace in the moment and look for the *big-picture* understanding of why things happen later.

I understand the power of grace because I didn't give myself any at that time. Two months after Eduardo's accident, I had transformed into a full-blown helicopter mom, following my baby closely for as many hours as my body could handle in a day. Eduardo was alive, and it had quickly become my life's mission to make sure he was safe at all times.

The doctors had been very clear: Edu had miraculously survived the accident, but there was still a lot of uncertainty about his recovery. The areas of his brain affected by the trauma controlled crucial bodily functions, from sleep patterns to fluid regulation and hormone production. My mission was to protect his precious life.

I meticulously recorded every possible signal that could provide information about his internal system, documenting every detail to share with the team of doctors who were closely monitoring his incredible recovery. I had to weigh his diapers every time he peed to make sure he didn't become dehydrated, and monitor his sleep periods, the color of his skin, the appearance of his eyes, his food and water intake, and all other bodily functions.

Everything had to be carefully monitored and shared with the team of doctors.

That's when I started to notice that some of his behaviors were different from other kids his age. He walked on his toes frequently, showed increased sensitivity to sound and light, and had problems with language development. He would also rock when he got anxious or would burst into a tearful tantrum. I realized that these symptoms had appeared long before the accident, but my son was alive, so I was going to do everything in my power to make sure we got through whatever came our way.

One day, we visited my grandmother Margarita, whom we called Mamama. She had unparalleled intuition and she was always in tune with the subtle energies of life. She silently watched Edu running around her house, seemingly struggling to make peace with the world around him. Mamama held my hands with infinite love and wisdom. She could see right into the depths of my soul and she gently told me, "It's time to get help, my love."

A part of me recognized the undeniable truth in her words. A part of me also recognized the incredible support I already received from my mom. Another part of me didn't want to be ungrateful to the Universe for giving my son a second chance at life, so I felt the need to gratefully embrace everything that came my way.

Mamama sensed the battle going on inside my mind and squeezed my hands tighter. With a tone of loving authority, she told me, "Take this $100 and get help, Francesca. I made an appointment for Eduardo with a neurodevelopmental specialist for tomorrow." There was no room for more arguments with my grandmother. I knew she was right. Something deeper was developing in my son's life, and I could no longer ignore it. Ignoring the truth was not going to help Edu at all.

I went to see the neurodevelopment specialist, and it was at that moment that I received the second major diagnosis of Eduardo's short life.

"He has Pervasive Developmental Disorder," said the specialist.
"And what does that mean?" I asked.
"It means he's on the autism spectrum..."

After that, I stopped listening to the doctor's words. All I could hear were my inner voices, all speaking to me at the same time at full volume. *Autism? This sounds surreal. Autism? This happens to other people but not to me. Autism? This is not fair! We've already been through so much! Autism? Is this a life sentence for him?*

For the next 45 minutes, my mind was flooded with an army of different scenarios, thinking about what could have caused this and what the future might hold. I felt an overwhelming need to cry and vomit at the same time.

Then, the image of the boy with the train came back to my mind, and my heart reminded me that when faced with something so immense, I could always ask for help. I began to calm down, silencing the echo of that second life sentence for my son. *These were only worst-case scenarios and did not predict our destiny. Not on my watch!* I committed to giving my son the best opportunities I could in life.

After the appointment with the neurodevelopmentalist, I began making calls to form a team of *superhero therapists* who would help my son live the best life possible. Within a week, I had scheduled appointments with a speech therapist, a behavior modification therapist, and a special education teacher. I ordered every autism book available on Amazon and was ready to kick autism's ass.

Over the next years, I dedicated eight hours a week to my son's therapy, becoming an *expert* on autism. I organized therapy sessions at home to reinforce what we learned from the specialists. I created a support network for his school, educating teachers, classmates, and everyone involved in Eduardo's daily life on how to coexist with autism. I went to every seminar available, read every book on autism, incorporated sensory integration therapy, and fought against people's bullying and ignorance at every corner of the journey. Everything in my life was programmed. Everything had to be carefully structured to help my son deal with the overwhelming reality of his condition.

He cried frequently as if the world hurt him. Certain sounds triggered him, making him frantically slap his tiny hands over his ears to stop the sensations he couldn't control. The textures on his skin often bothered him, leading me to cut every tag off of his clothing to alleviate his discomfort. He also had problems with some textures and colors of his food, so I had to carefully regulate his diet. Edu never took a nap nor slept through the night. His system constantly interrupted his sleep, and there came a point where I simply surrendered to the chaos, crying with him during his midnight sorrows.

He wouldn't let me hug him to comfort him, so I stayed next to him, feeling completely helpless. I knew that I had to gather my strength and be the pillar of support for him. It was my responsibility to help him. I just needed to figure out how. Therapy was often a difficult process, filled with cries of pain as the specialists tried to guide Edu through his struggles. I could see how difficult the sessions were for him and how difficult it was to have to continue these therapies at home every day.

Two years after starting the therapeutic process, I knew I had to do something more to help my son. While the therapies were good for him, they were moving too slowly, so I decided to incorporate a holistic approach to help speed things up, starting with a change in his diet. I eliminated gluten, casein, sugars, and dyes from his diet, wanting to cleanse his body of anything that could harm it and, in doing so, help his nervous system cope better with the world. I had to educate everyone who came into contact with my son to understand that removing the cake from Edu's life was not torture, but rather much-needed medicine.

I come from a large Latin family where food is one of the ways we show love, so I experienced a lot of resistance, but I stood my ground for the sake of my son. A couple of months after changing his diet, I started to see substantial progress. Eduardo finally began sleeping through the night, looked more serene, experienced a complete transformation in his digestive system, and began forming complete sentences. This transformation began to take place when Eduardo was 5 years old. He no longer screamed when I held him for short periods, and he could cope much better with external sounds.

Exhausted by this relentless battle, I felt like I had finally discovered the key to effectively supporting my son on his unique journey. The feeling of relief was immense, although I knew that the journey was just beginning. At this point, I was ready to start building the next chapter of my life.

Journal Insight Questions and Action Steps

Are you one of those people who are very hard on yourself? If you said yes, then this exercise is exactly for you! The point of this reflection practice is for you to recognize and honor that you are human, and learn to give yourself grace.

- Go back to your list of Kensho moments from the last chapter and reflect on your internal chatter at the time. The moments where you were hard on yourself, or you wished that you had done or said something differently.
- Take a deep breath and notice how you treat yourself when life presents you with a big challenge.
- Now go back to those situations and see them from the perspective of a loving human. Imagine those situations happen to someone you love, and they are the ones being hard on themselves. What would you say to them? What can you see when someone else is going through a rough patch and feels they are not doing enough, or not doing it right?
- Feel all that love and grace for **YOU**.

"I can't tell you the key to success, but the key to failure is trying to please everyone."

– Ed Sheeran

CHAPTER 4

WHEN YOU NEGLECT YOURSELF

*I*n the vast majority of cultures, women are set as the primary caregivers, nurturers, and caretakers by nature, while men are usually seen as the providers. This model of the world has been like this for millennia, from our ancestral hunter-gatherer tribes where men went out to hunt and women took care of the tribe and the food preparation. Even though things have changed a lot throughout our human history, and we now have more shared roles as men and women, there are still many of these old models tightly installed in our consciousness.

I have worked with thousands of people from all over the globe in my years as a coach and have listened to hundreds of stories from women who, in their effort of trying to fit a certain model of the society that they were born in, end up forgetting about their own wants and needs to please others. And this operation can only be sustained for a limited time. You can put on a *mask* to hide your emotions under the rug and try to live by the labels and expectations of others for a while, but if you neglect your core, all the carefully built layers that you put on top of the other throughout the years will eventually crumble.

It is really beautiful when you want to serve others. It is the most amazing privilege that you get to give with an open heart to the people you love, but you have to *fill your tank first* if you want this to be sustainable. You have to love and care for yourself with the same intensity that you do for others.

If you have ever been on a plane, you will easily understand this.

Right before takeoff, you will see a flight attendant give you a set of instructions on how to keep yourself and others safe in case of an emergency. One of the most important directions is to *"Put your mask on first."* When you put on your mask first, you will be able to protect your integrity first, and that will allow you to help others in case they needed. We *know this*, and yet somehow, we tend to ignore it. I know this from personal experience.

If you had met me before 2016, you would have found a very different person than the one you see today. To those who knew me, my life seemed to align seamlessly with the ideals of perfection defined by all of society's external standards. But beneath that perfect external image, I was feeling a lot of pain and frustration. I had fully committed myself to please others in all areas of my life and had made it my personal mission to *save* everyone and improve their lives. But while trying to be a *"Perfect Human"* for everyone else, I forgot about myself.

It all started after my three-year relationship with my then-boyfriend when I decided to get married again and extend my family. Throughout the accident and Edu's autism diagnosis, Adrián had been a very important support in my life, and we wanted to build our future together. We got married in the spring of 2002, and my daughter Ana Victoria (Avi) was born in the winter of that same year. My son Edu was 4 years old and Adrián's daughter, Camila, was 6. We finally had the big family we both wanted, and I finally experienced the feeling of having a *normal* family life.

Adrián was a man of rigid routines and preferences. He was 16 years older than me and was used to living alone, so I adapted to his way of life and his needs. He had embraced Eduardo as his own son. They loved each other from the first time they met, and Adrián had fought to become his father. I celebrated having my own family and felt like all the pieces of my life were finally falling into place. I was dedicated to my home and my children. My days were carefully organized to make sure I could take care of every aspect of our lives, so the life of my dreams that I had fought so hard to create could continue to thrive.

My daughter Avi was a force of nature from the day she came out of my womb; she radiated insatiable curiosity and boundless energy. She spent her first years accompanying me to Edu's multiple therapies. She learned to crawl and then walk into one of the many therapy waiting rooms we spent so much time in.

After years of this routine, I wanted to give Avi her own space outside of her brother's therapies so she could explore what she loved. I enrolled Avi in dance when she was 3 years old, and after six years of dancing, she was invited to join the Dance Company, which meant a greater commitment for us. This included more hours of practice, international competitions, and more expenses. But she deserved the same love and attention that I had given my son, so I committed to supporting her and scheduling her dreams on my calendar.

Eventually, we got a bigger house near a great school and Adrian's workplace. I got a second job to help pay the mounting bills that supported our lifestyle, and I carefully crafted my calendar to accommodate all my commitments including taking Edu to therapies, taking Avi to dance, and being a mother, wife, and worker... This had been my dream after all, and I was determined to do whatever it took to keep it. All my waking hours were allocated to serving others. I was determined to make things great for my family, and I would fight for the quality of life of my loved ones with every cell in my body.

This is what my daily schedule looked like:

- 6:00 am: Rise, prepare breakfast, and get my kids ready for school.
- 7:00 am: Drop my kids off at school and head to my first job.
- Noon: Return home to prepare lunch for my husband and catch up on my second job.
- 2:30 pm: Pick up my kids from school, feed them, help with homework, and prepare for therapy sessions and dance lessons.
- 3:30 pm: Drive to therapy and dance lessons. Work while I wait for my kids.
- 7:00 pm: Return home to prepare dinner and include some "quality" family time.
- 8:30 pm: Tuck my kids into bed.
- 9:30 pm: Quality time with my husband.
- 10:00 pm: Finish reviewing the pending work for my two jobs.

- 11:00 pm: Finally, I'd have a moment to myself before crashing to sleep, only to repeat the cycle the next day.

This busy schedule was repeated from Monday to Friday for years. To ensure that I wouldn't break down under so much pressure, my mother took my children to sleep at her house every Friday, which allowed me to get a few precious extra hours of rest on Saturday mornings. This was the key to staying sane and not breaking down for so long.

Sundays were family days, and we often spent them outside the house. We usually went to family gatherings where I ended up babysitting our three children, while Adrian participated in the *adult* section of the party, enjoying the drinks. We ended Sundays with me dragging my husband back home so we could put our kids to bed and get at least six hours of sleep before it all started again the next day.

I tried to do my best and keep a smile on my face, but there were some days when I felt like my strength was leaving me. I desperately needed a break, but I felt so guilty for wanting it! My inner voice always told me phrases like: *"You can do more. You chose this, so now suck it up."* I never knew I had other options at that time in my life. I just thought this was what normal life was like for a married woman with children. That this was my *normal* and I had to do everything I could to make it work.

Journal Insight Questions and Action Steps

- Think about your own life and make a list of the daily activities that you routinely do.
- From that list, note what fills you with energy and what drains your energy.
- Think about some of the ways for you to let go of the activities that make you feel drained. Like delegating them to someone else, asking for help, or simply stop doing them altogether.
- Then reflect on some of the practices that you can start incorporating in your days that will serve YOU. How will you *"Put your mask on first"*?

CHAPTER 5

BREAKING
DOWN

The *"Breaking Point"* is a raw experience that you can't ignore. When you get here, every single cell in your body will scream to let you know the *point of no return* has arrived. This usually happens after you have added layers and layers of new responsibilities that you think you *should* add to your life until the bubble of heaviness explodes in your face.

This will usually come as a result of you neglecting your wants and needs for a prolonged time, which causes emotional, physical, and mental exhaustion that leads to burnout. This happens after a long time of having a greater output (what you give to others) than an input (what you give to yourself).

Breaking is both a chaotic and delicious experience. Think of it like shedding your old skin to allow your new *self* to emerge. It may be a difficult time in your life, as is the case with every major transition, but it is the only way to free yourself from old patterns that must be shattered before your *true self* can blossom.

To understand this, think of an iguana.

Iguanas, like many other reptiles, shed their skin as a natural part of their growth and development process:

- **Growth**: They need to shed their skin because it doesn't grow with them, so they need to let go of their old skin and replace it with new, larger skin.

- *Release*: Shedding helps them release any old or damaged layers so they can maintain the integrity and function of their skin (which is to protect them).
- *Discomfort*: Releasing their old skin is an uncomfortable process that requires a focused effort, but they know it's worth it and do it anyway.

I really love the simplicity of life's lessons taught by nature. Such a powerful reminder that breaking is a completely normal process for any being. Including YOU.

This is the story of how I finally broke under pressure. At that point in my life, all my days ran like a Swiss clock. Each piece was carefully designed to complement each other. One of these pieces was the school I had chosen for my children, which was not only 300 meters from our house but was also very aligned with what me and my husband wanted for our children's future.

Edu and Avi had spent their entire lives at the same school, and everyone knew them inside and out. At that time, Edu was 13 years old and Avi was 9. I had worked closely with the school for many years, spending countless hours training staff, students, and even parents about autism. After years of tireless work, it seemed that everything was working *perfectly*.

But the Universe has a great sense of humor and always fills you with surprises. In the moment, it might feel like a punch in the gut, but oftentimes, you later realize that they were actually meant to serve you. This *punch* is usually unexpected and extremely uncomfortable as that is the point of it: to shake you awake from something that's not serving you anymore.

I received the *punch* at my son's school.

When Edu graduated from sixth grade, I was called to a meeting with the school's psychology department, a department I had met with monthly for years. They celebrated Edu's achievement in finishing primary school, thanked me for all my contributions as a mother, and then dropped a bomb on me.

"What are your plans for Eduardo's future?" the psychologist asked me. I was completely dazzled by the question.

"What do you mean?" I asked

"I mean, where are you going to take him to high school?"

"I am not planning on changing schools for him," I said, matter-of-factly.

"I'm sorry, Miss Facio, but he is not prepared for our high school system. You have to look for another school," the psychologist said.

FUUUUUUUUUUCCCKKKKKKKKKKK! I was so angry, that all I could think about was throwing a punch right into the wall. That blow hit me so hard! What did she mean, *"He was not ready for their school?"* *Oh really!?* We had been meeting every week for years; I had invested all my love and energy into that school, and now they were telling me I had to take him somewhere else. *WHAT*???

My inner warrior wanted to fight. I knew this was unfair. I had done *EVERYTHING* right. I was going to meetings, I was going to therapy, I was fully involved, I was working two jobs to cover all the bills, and I was using every minute of my day to make things work…and now this. This was *NOT FAIR*. How much more shit was I supposed to receive in one lifetime? I just wanted to punch the walls and scream. But I realized that anger and frustration wouldn't fix anything, and I had to find another way forward. After all, the Universe had given my son a second chance at life, so I had to *suck it up* and keep fighting.

For the next four years, I diligently completed my to-do list with a resignation born from struggling for so long. But part of me had stopped believing that things were going to get better. The hopeful part of me began to wither under the bureaucracy of life. So I moved on, focusing on the next task at hand, and pushing myself to get through the day. The constant calls from the bank reminded us every day that we were behind on our mortgage payments. I felt perpetually exhausted amidst the overwhelming responsibilities related to the house, my husband, my children, and juggling two jobs.

Although my mother was my greatest support during these times, I felt that joy was escaping my being, and that is how I began to drink every night to numb my worries. No matter how hard we tried, the money was never enough. I tried to do the best I could, but it was never enough. My mind sang a relentless chorus of *never enough*.

Then, one Friday afternoon, March 11, 2016, I drove in my husband's car to the bank to try to come to an agreement and stop the endless reminders of *"it's not enough"*. My mind was so full of thoughts that I got distracted in the parking lot and crashed my husband's car into a wall. At that moment, all my will to fight left my body, preparing it to release all the tears I had so carefully suppressed over the years. I took the wrecked car home and allowed myself to cry. The floodgates were open, and I couldn't stop my body from letting go of the years of stored frustration I had accumulated.

That Friday night, I finally allowed my 37-year-old *self* to break through the barriers of control and simply let go. Alone on my terrace, sitting in the company of a bottle of wine, I allowed myself to cry with the same intensity as the storm that was opening in the heavens. That night, I finally screamed at the sky. That night I finally asked God for some kind of help for ME.

"There has to be more to life than this!" I screamed at the sky. "Please show me what I'm supposed to do!"

That was the moment I stopped being in *perpetual warrior mode* and surrendered to the Universe. Not because I wanted to, but because I was exhausted from fighting and didn't know what else to do. As I relinquished control, my heartbeat began to slow. The constant mental chatter filled with horrible thoughts finally stopped. As I breathed along with the steady rain, my heart found a moment of peace, releasing the heavy burden of responsibilities and embracing the possibility of receiving.

The next day, I opened my e-mail to find exactly what I had asked for…

Journal Insight Questions

- Do you feel like you can continue your current lifestyle and list of to-do's like it is right now for the next 10-20 years?
- What is the most important thing that you need and want for yourself right now?
- If you could ask the Universe for anything and KNOW that you would get it, what would you ask for?

PART 2

THE INVITATION:
START TO LOOK FOR YOUR FEATHERS

When you think about the hero's journey in every story ever
told, there is always a point in the story where there is an
invitation that completely changes the course of the hero's life.

The invitation is about burning the bridges behind you
—learning to trust fully in the path ahead.

This is the beginning of the most incredible adventure of your life,
taking you on a journey to rediscover who
you really are and connect you
with what your soul is meant to do on this planet.

The invitation calls you to shed the restrictive
layers built up over years of conditioning
so that you can create your life on your own terms,
remembering that something amazing awaits
you on the other side of fear.

Once you accept the Invitation, you will
embark on a personal treasure hunt
to look for the magic in your everyday life: YOUR FEATHERS.

Feathers that can be found in the little moments of your days
if you are willing and open to seeing them.

Feathers that will help you build the wings that you have
dormant at your back, that are waiting for you to awaken
them from the long slumber that will allow you to fly.

CHAPTER 6

YOUR
PERSONAL
HONEYMOON

*W*hen you embark on a journey to redesign your life, you need a moment to reconnect with who you *are* first. Changing the course of your reality can be exciting, but it will also require all your strength. Taking a moment to pause and reflect on what you want to create is essential. And I know what you are thinking: *"I have so many things I have to take care of right now, how can I possibly take some time just for me?"* Or *"What will my loved ones do if I take some time for myself, isn't that selfish?"*

NO, it isn't selfish.

The most powerful thing that you can do for yourself and everyone you care for is to *love* yourself first. You need to make space to *fill your tank* and nourish your soul. This allows you to create from a place of infinite possibilities and not from a place of tired limitations. Because before you can fully give to others, you need to fill your emotional tank first!

Imagine that you have a Porsche. A new beautiful car capable of running at incredible speed and performing outstandingly on any road. But you never take care of it. You use diesel instead of premium gas, and you forget to check the oil. No matter how good the car is built to be, if you don't take care of it, it will eventually break. The same happens with you. So a personal honeymoon is not an act of selfishness; it is actually very far from that.

When you learn how to prioritize yourself first, you are not only teaching others how to do it for themselves, but you are also reminding yourself and your loved ones that everyone is powerful enough to create a life on their terms. This *sacred pause* is essential for everyone's survival, but this is also one of the most powerful ways to thrive. Our bodies are not meant to be running in high gear all of the time—this creates exhaustion. Our minds require *brain breaks* to recharge. This is our *normal* state of being, but we have forgotten about this because we live in a world that has us on high alert 24/7.

Think about a regular honeymoon. Imagine two people who decided to start their lives together, and they take some time away from the world to celebrate their love, get to know one another more deeply, and share their hopes and dreams about the future that they are going to create together. Everything is bliss; they are in sync with one another, enjoying all the little moments that come. Time seems to fly because they are completely submerged in the experience.

Sounds amazing, right?

This is exactly what a personal honeymoon is. The only difference is that the person that you take with you is not separate from yourself. The person that you get to know on a deeper level, the one that you will devote all of your love and attention to, is *you*.

Let me share more of my story so you can see how I used a personal honeymoon to recreate my life anew. This is the story of how I was finally able to make time for myself for the first time in 17 years after starting my journey as a mom. The first time that I permitted myself to embark on a journey that was only meant to nurture myself. This was the answer that I received when I asked the Universe to help ME on that rainy Friday night.

One of my two jobs during that period of my life was as manager of Mindvalley's customer service department for the Costa Rican unit. Saturday morning after I asked the Universe for a sign of *something else,* I sat down at my computer to check my emails before my family woke up. There was an email in my inbox that immediately caught my attention. It was an invitation from Vishen, the owner of Mindvalley, who asked me to come to the Mindvalley main offices in Kuala Lumpur for a whole month because he wanted to meet with all the managers of his different departments. I stared at the email for a long time without being able to move. It scared me how incredibly detailed the answer to my pleas was.

How quickly the Universe had answered me! WOW!

A part of me was incredibly grateful and excited for the opportunity to go away for an entire month *alone*. But another part of me was terrified at the thought of putting all my responsibilities on hold to focus only on myself. All the images of the disasters that could happen if I abandoned my carefully constructed *family operation* came flooding back to me: *Who would take care of my children? Who would take Edu to therapy and Avi to dance rehearsals? Who was going to take care of the housework?* And on top of everything, I was completely broke at that time.

I took a deep breath to calm my fears and continued reading the email. It said that not only would they cover my plane ticket, but they would also give me a place to stay for the entire month. All I had to do was get there. It sounded too good to be true. But that was exactly what I had asked the Universe for—a sign, something to show me my way. I had asked for a pause, a break, a real honeymoon with myself! A whole month, just for ME, leaving my to-dos in Costa Rica for a while.

For 17 years, I had been a *super mom,* a *super wife,* and a super responsible person who juggled two jobs. I was the therapist at home, the unconditional friend, the sister, and the leader of a growing team. I was many things to many people, but I had neglected my inner woman. In all those years, I had put my own needs on hold to serve others, as I believed *"I should."* I hadn't even considered taking some time for myself.

Until that day. Until that email.

My inner fear and excitement called me to an emergency meeting within myself to discuss this opportunity in my head. I heard my thoughts talking frantically at the same time:

Fear: "Who will take care of my children while I am gone? How will they take care of themselves?

Emotion: "Everyone deserves time off, and I am not alone. I can ask for help!"

Fear: "I'm broke and I have too many responsibilities."

Emotion: "But I need some time for myself!"

Fear: "What is my husband going to say?"

Emotion: "This IS my job and I have to go. I actually WANT and need some time for myself. PERIOD."

Thank God, my excitement drowned out the voice of my fear, and I emailed Vishen with a resounding **YES**. I closed my computer with my hands still shaking, but knowing that this lifeboat was a once-in-a-lifetime opportunity. My family was shocked when I told them the news of my trip. My husband had no idea what he had to do. My children couldn't understand why I was leaving. It felt like the world had suddenly stopped for everyone, except my mom, who quickly offered to help me, like she always did.

Leaving aside my family's mental turmoil, I had already said yes. My bags were packed, and this trip was a reality. My family had a week to figure out how to navigate life without me, and all I could do was pray that everyone would be alive and well when I returned.

When I said goodbye to my children at the airport, my heart felt heavy with guilt. However, another part of me recognized that this work trip, this *mom vacation,* was essential to our collective survival.

Crossing the customs threshold was when I realized there was no turning back. My heart started beating faster and stronger with every step I took. My adventure was beginning. A giant smile graced my face as I launched myself into the unknown. It was a smile that never left during the next 36 hours of flights toward that new adventure of rediscovering who I was.

When I finally arrived at my apartment in Kuala Lumpur, I freshened up a bit, left my suitcases on the bed, and went out to discover the city. My body was full of energy, and I was ultra-aware. Every little detail became clear and crisp. I could notice EVERYTHING, absorbing everything. The beautiful blue sky above my head, the jasmine tree growing in the middle of the sidewalk that smelled like heaven, the bright sun above me. With gratitude in my heart, I welcomed it all.

My heart was pounding with anticipation, and I asked the Universe for guidance to make the most of this honeymoon with myself. I asked for a sign, an anchor to guide the course of my experience. When I arrived at the Mindvalley headquarters and opened the office doors, I saw it clearly.

Mindvalley's logo is a pair of wings. I had seen these wings countless times, but now they had a completely new and different meaning. That was going to be the goal of that month—to find my feathers, rebuild my wings, and learn to fly again. At that moment, I decided that I would ferociously search for my feathers in every corner and every experience I would have for the next 30 days.

A warm tribe welcomed me into the office. Vibrant young people radiated hope and energy. They reminded me of the woman I had hidden in a box before motherhood, before marriage, before work: *the woman I was before the labels.*

This was the first feather I found for my wings.

Journal Insight Questions and Action Steps

Design your Personal Honeymoon

- Imagine that you have everything you need at your disposal right now: money, time and all the help you need to take some time just for you. Imagine you are taking a personal honeymoon with yourself.
- Paint a clear picture of your Personal Honeymoon. Make sure you incorporate all your senses into this vision and get as clear as possible!

You can use the questions below to expand on your vision:

- Why do you want/ need this? Why is this important for you?
- Where would you go? What is the location that is calling you? Is it a beach? A mountain? What location comes to mind?
- For how long?
- What would you love to do for yourself? What are the activities that you really enjoy? What are the things you want to explore?
- How do you want to feel throughout your personal honeymoon?
- What do you want to experience? Is it an adventure? Calmness?
- Then allow yourself to soak this in for the next 20 minutes.

Results of Your Personal Honeymoon

- How will your life benefit after you take time for yourself? What will happen to your health? Your emotional well-being? Your mindset?
- How will the lives of the people around you benefit as well?

Action Steps You Can Take Today

- What are some of the things that you describe in your personal honeymoon that you can do for yourself TODAY? You can start with something small, like doing some breathing exercises, soaking your feet in warm water, getting a massage, going out for a walk, finding a new hobby, etc.
- Make a list of that and start to incorporate some of these things in your weekly schedule today.

CHAPTER 7

WHAT DO
YOU WANT?

*U*sually, the simplest questions are the most difficult to answer. We spend countless hours dreaming of a life that exists outside of the complications we impose on ourselves, but we rarely stop to ask ourselves what it is we *really* want. Only when we can pause and truly connect with our hearts will we finally be able to see the answer.

We usually have a *mental movie* that comes to mind when we reflect on what we really want for ourselves, but this *mental movie* tends to be blurry. This usually happens to all of us people pleasers who are always thinking about everyone else before ourselves, until there comes a point in our lives where it gets difficult to distinguish what we want amid everyone else's needs.

Having a personal vision of that ideal life gives your soul a *North Star*, a place that you want to get to if everything goes according to *plan*. Once you know clearly what that is, then it's a lot easier for you to get there. It's essential to get very clear on who you want to BE, what you want to experience in each area of your life, and what you need to incorporate into your everyday life to get there.

To understand what you want, you need to *turn down the voice of your ego* and give your heart a voice for a change. Your ego is the voice that is constantly trying to protect you from perceived danger and doesn't let you hear your truth. But everything starts with that connection with your core. With who you really ARE. Once you achieve this, everything else becomes more clear.

The Universe is **ABUNDANT** and willing to give you exactly what you ask for. All you have to do is get clear on what that is. As humans, we tend to spend too much time focusing on what we don't want and we forget to pay attention to the things that we **DO** want.

Let that sink in for a minute.

When you can name what you want to create for yourself, your *Reticular Activation System* (this is like a brain GPS) will start to scan your surroundings to bring that thing to reality. So in this chapter, I invite you to consciously decide what you want so you can start to look for your unique feathers. Feathers that you will use to create your own set of wings.

Let me tell you how that happened to me when I got clear on what I wanted…

Kuala Lumpur was a completely different world compared to my reality in Costa Rica. It was a tapestry woven from diverse cultures and ethnicities, a place where grand skyscrapers coexisted with ancient temples, and where the symphony of global cuisines and sounds harmonized in one place. It was a delicious trip for my senses.

The day after my arrival, I headed to the Mindvalley office feeling like Wendy embarking on her adventure to Neverland. The morning meeting, held in a tree house, was nothing short of magical. Sitting in a circle on oversized pillows, we began to have a conversation about the day, which turned into the vision for the next month, and somehow, we arrived at the vision we had for our lives. One of my young colleagues asked me a question that changed everything for me. She asked me: "What do you want, Fran?"

It was such a simple question and yet one that had such a profound effect on me. "*What do I want?*" I hadn't thought about this question in years. In fact, I didn't remember the last time I had asked myself what I wanted. Not what my children or my husband wanted, but **ME**. My heart was happy because it would finally get a place at the table of my inner thoughts. It was finally getting its voice back. I spent the rest of the day thinking about that question. It was so big that I didn't know how to respond. All I knew was that I had to allow it to unveil itself in its own time.

The first thing I decided on my personal honeymoon was that I would not cook, clean, or serve a single meal during my entire trip. I set out to explore the delicious culinary options Kuala Lumpur had to offer, immersing myself in different restaurants and cafes, and making connections with new people along the way. It felt liberating! I had no idea that such a small decision could have such a significant impact on my sense of freedom.

Another feather for my wings.

During that first week in Kuala Lumpur, we received incredible news. A couple named Jon and Missy Butcher had created a methodology to help people design their ideal life. This methodology was called Lifebook, and they wanted to bring it into the Mindvalley educational ecosystem. As we normally test our programs before offering them to others, all Mindvalley employees were invited to participate in their weekend workshop. Lifebook was one of those life-changing programs that I had been long waiting for without even knowing it.

Throughout that weekend, I entered into a holistic reflection of my life. I spent the entire weekend reflecting on my life as a whole. For the first time, I incorporated all areas of myself, not just my motherhood, my career, and my relationships, but what I *really* wanted for my health, what I wanted to experience in my life, and how I wanted to grow. I finally gained clarity on the path I wanted to take for my life. What my legacy would look and feel like. I allowed myself to dream bigger than ever, while I asked all limitations to leave my reality.

An inner power that had been dormant for a long time suddenly awakened within me. I recognized that creating my ideal life was much easier than I had ever imagined. I was **completely committed**, ready to mold the "*Plasticine*" that the Universe was giving me in abundance.

I invite you to take your own Lifebook assessment to see how you are doing in all areas of your life at: **https://life.mindvalley.com**.

Having a map of where you are today can help you be clear about where you want to be tomorrow!

Journal Insight Questions & Action Steps

- When you think about your future, write what you would love to create (your ideal vision) in these different areas of your life:
    - **Your health** - How you want to look and feel in your body: vitality, fitness, mobility, mental clarity.
    - **Emotional life** - Your emotional well-being: self-awareness, emotional intelligence, relationship, and managing emotions effectively.
    - **Spirituality** - All about connectedness: your beliefs, values, purpose, and life mission.
    - **Family** - This is all about your important relationships with your closest family members, like your children, parents, and siblings.
    - **Love relationship** - Focuses on romantic relationships: communication, intimacy, trust, and shared goals with a partner.
    - **Social life** - Meaningful connections: relationships with friends, colleagues, and your community.
    - **Intellect** - Focuses on the pursuit of knowledge and skills: what you want to learn, and how you want to grow.
    - **Finances** - Your relationship with money and abundance: income, savings, investments, budgeting, and long-term financial goals.
- Why is it important for you to achieve your ideal vision for each one of these areas?
- What are some of the things you can start implementing TODAY to get closer to your ideal vision for each area of your life?
- What are other ways for you to achieve your ideal vision for all areas of your life in the next 3-5 years? Strategies that you can implement for the long term.
- Write down some strategies you can use or skills you can learn.

CHAPTER 8

RELEASE THE
URGE TO
CONTROL
EVERYTHING

*W*e humans have a natural tendency to want to keep things under control. This *urge* is deeply rooted in our human nature and comes from many different factors related to our psychology, social upbringing, and evolutionary development.

- *Psychology* - As humans, we want to feel safe, especially in a world filled with uncertainty. We also want to avoid emotions that feel uncomfortable, like fear. Control can also fulfill various psychological needs, such as the need for autonomy ("I have a choice"), competence ("I can do this"), and relatedness ("This is important for me")
- *Social upbringing* - *Having control* over your life is celebrated by our culture. People who are unsure of where they are going are usually viewed as clueless, and people with detailed plans are usually celebrated.
- *Evolution* - The sense of *having control* is directly linked to our survival instinct because we had to keep ourselves safe from

the many threats that we faced in our distant past. We also had
to control our access to the resources we needed to survive.

The desire to control what happens outside of you is an *illusion*.
There is no possible way that you can control anything that happens outside **YOU**. You just can't! So understand that although wanting control
is part of your human nature, it is not something that you can do. This
is the first step to allow you to relax into the experiences that come your
way. With this, I am not saying that you release control of everything and
leave your entire *life operation* to chance. It is good to have order in your
life and create accountability systems that work for you. I mean this just
as an invitation for you to be open to experiencing the moment, even if
it's not in perfect alignment with your *plan*.

Imagine this as having an *"Internal Waze"* - your internal guiding
system.

In the last chapter, you gained more clarity on what you want to
create in the most important areas of your life (this is like typing the
destination of where you want to go). This chapter is about releasing
control. This is allowing your *Internal Guiding System* to guide your trip
through life while you are part of co-creating your reality.

When you learn to let go of the expectations of what can happen, then you can start to enjoy what each situation of life brings
you. And when you do that, you can welcome the adventure of trusting what is coming, even if you don't know what it is. And this is
possible, believe me! I had a master's degree in wanting to control
everything around me. This was because I was raised to believe that
women should manage all the *heavy load* of everyone's life. It was also
from my experience of being a mother and wanting to avoid anything
bad happening to my loved ones.

It was during my personal honeymoon that I was able to experience the huge relief of letting go of control for a while. It was a liberating sensation—and one I got to feel for the very first time during my
time in Kuala Lumpur. The week following my Lifebook experience, I
began to connect more deeply with myself and my energy. As I settled
into life in Kuala Lumpur, I learned to trust the idea that everything
at home was fine. For the first time in a long time, I felt like I had

permission to live for myself. The guilt felt like a distant memory from a whole different person.

On a Thursday afternoon at the office, we met as usual to celebrate our accomplishments of the week. We called it the *"A-report,"* and following this celebration of shared achievements, we closed with a social gathering. We were sharing stories and chilling out with other colleagues when suddenly, my friend Ericka approached me in the middle of the celebrations. She was smiling as she asked me a question: *"What is your biggest dream, Fran?"*

What a delicious question to think about! It was a question I had never allowed myself to consider before that trip, but after a full week on my honeymoon, and having had the opportunity to connect with what I wanted, it suddenly occurred to me: "I would love to visit Cambodia and see the sunrise at Angkor Wat!" I said this without hesitation. There was something about Cambodia that seemed magical but distant to me. I could vividly imagine myself at that moment admiring the sunrise atop that ancient temple.

Ericka smiled and said, "Let's go tomorrow!"

My heart skipped a beat and my muscles tensed. "Are you crazy?" I exclaimed.

"Let's do it," she responded enthusiastically. "Come on!"

My inner perfectionist sprang into action, clutching her chest into a would-be heart attack. *What on earth was my friend thinking? It was nearly midnight, we had made no plans, and last I checked, a trip to Cambodia was super expensive. Plus, I was practically broke. This was insane!* My friend simply smiled as I engaged in my internal battle. She grabbed my credit card, walked to a computer, and bought my $100 ticket to Cambodia.

"There, it's done," she declared. "You leave tomorrow at 11 am."

For a few seconds, I couldn't move. Everything had happened effortlessly for her. She had made a decision and acted on it, without overthinking or allowing her inner doubts to sabotage her. Suddenly, $100 didn't seem like such a terrible thing. *It was a very different figure than the $2,500 it would have cost me to travel from Costa Rica to Cambodia. Plus, did I really need much for a long weekend?*

I had a few hours to pack, but that was no longer a problem for me. I left the office that night feeling lighter than I had in years. I laughed like crazy as I walked back to my apartment at midnight, excited to fulfill one of my biggest dreams without getting attached to the *how*. I quickly put together a bag with whatever I could find in my closet, left it near the door, and lay down on my bed to imagine my adventure. Of course, I couldn't sleep that night. My mind was too active and my heart was too loud, racing at a million miles. I didn't care about not sleeping; all I could think about was the magical place I was about to visit. What an extraordinary way to let go of fear!

Cambodia was everything I had imagined but in a very different way.

At the airport, I was warmly greeted by "Papa," a man in his 60s with sun-beaten skin and a perennial smile. He was a kind soul who would become our driver and guide during our stay in Siem Reap. Papa spoke little English and I couldn't speak Khmer at all, but somehow, we communicated through the power of his energy and radiant smile. He drove a tuk-tuk, which was basically a motorcycle attached to a wooden box with seats and wheels, without windows or a seat belt. I got into the tuk-tuk and let myself be enveloped in the experience.

On the 30-minute ride from the airport to my hotel, I witnessed a completely different reality. Cambodians drive at incredible speed and in every direction imaginable. The motorcycles carry loads several times their size without dropping anything; you see groups of four people traveling on a motorcycle and buses packed with twice the number of passengers allowed, many of them on the roof. It was a chaotic dance that, by some miraculous alignment of the forces of life, allowed everyone to move through the city without dying.

When I arrived at my hotel, I was overcome with relief and gratitude for having made it there alive. My friends Ericka and Hazel were already waiting for me, having arrived on a previous flight. They escorted me to my room, a tiny space decorated with vibrant colors and a small fan. I scanned the room, looking for the bathroom to freshen up, only to realize there was none. Ericka started laughing and directed me to the shared bathroom in the corner of the building. Part of me had to know that $10 a night wouldn't get me a five-star hotel, but I'd never experienced staying in a hostel, so it was all new to me.

I dropped my expectations on top of the bed, and we rented some bikes to explore the city of Siem Reap. Once you understood that cars honked at you just before they were about to hit you and that they even ran onto the sidewalk when traffic was heavy, you adapted and blended into the unique rhythm of the city. We found an incredible street lined with jasmine trees on both sides, and the fragrance of its flowers enveloped us. It was a sublime sensory experience.

I had already collected many feathers for my wings; so many gifts of life with every step we took. I felt incredibly alive, fully present, and incredibly grateful. I finally understood that life is meant to be lived in spurts of small magical moments. We spent the afternoon at the local market, blending seamlessly with the Cambodians, cycling around the city as if we had lived there for years.

Papa arrived at 4 am the next day to take us to Angkor Wat, where we hoped to see the sunrise. It was pitch black when we got there, but the sky was filled with thousands and thousands of stars, which reminded me how small we are in the Universe and how small our problems are compared to the immensity of creation. There was a large group of people from all over the world waiting to receive the sunrise in this mystical place. We gathered in front of the main temple, coffee in hand, conversation, and laughter as the backdrop to the scene, eagerly anticipating the spectacle of the sun.

And then we saw it!

The sound of conversations began to diminish and became a silent awe, as we watched the small globe of light rising between the two main columns of the temple. It was an impressive thing to see, and you could feel everyone's hearts beating together as we watched this gift of life. I finally understood what it felt like to be fully present. I finally understood why ancient civilizations worshiped the sun as one of their gods. It was such a magnificent sight; I was amazed. I let myself become completely immersed in that moment and noticed all the feathers that I had collected because of that.

Journal Insight Questions and Action Steps

- ***Find your triggers***: Write down 3-5 specific situations in your life where you feel a strong urge to control. These could be related to work, relationships, or personal goals.
- ***Note your reaction***: Write next to each situation how you tend to react when things don't go according to your plan.
  - o For example, you may feel anxious about a result and take over the task yourself or start to micromanage the other person.
- ***Find the root***: Now write why you feel like you need to control those situations.
  - o How does that make you feel?
  - o What result do you expect from exerting control?
- ***Change the perspective***: Write some alternative ways that you have to deal with each situation.
  - o For example, you can trust that the other person will deliver a result in their own way, or you can trust that things will unfold the best way possible without you controlling every aspect.
- ***Release***: Let go of the things that you cannot control; this includes everything that happens outside of you.
  - o Allow yourself to feel what you need to feel in the moment.
- ***Practice***: Practice checking in with yourself periodically every time you feel the urge to control a situation.
  - o Take a deep breath and choose how you want to respond that serves YOU.

CHAPTER 9

EXPLORE NEW
POSSIBILITIES

*O*ne of the most expansive exercises that I practice with my coaching clients is when I ask them to play. The sense of play and discovery is something that we knew how to easily do when we were children, and most of us forget it as we transition into adulthood even though it is one of the most liberating things you can do for yourself.

Imagine for a moment that you are an explorer in a new and distant land. You are the first person ever to set foot in this place, and all you have to do is explore freely before you can report back what you see. You get to this land and almost everything is new to you. Even though you recognize some of the plants in this place, there are many different animals that you have never seen, and you don't know the geography, but you feel excited to discover what this place brings you. Feel that in your body for a minute.

This is a fun way to get out of *your box* and open yourself to explore new possibilities. If you approach your life as an explorer, you are open to seeing life from a different lens. You become more aware of your present, you release the urge to control the experience, and you simply allow yourself to notice the many gifts that are just waiting to be witnessed by you.

When you allow yourself to play, suddenly your ego allows new information to pass through *the wall of protection* of your mind. This allows you to feel different, receive new information, and discover insights. But for you to be able to explore new possibilities, you have to give yourself permission first. Permission to experience what comes, trusting that everything that is presented to you is there for a reason. This permits you to think outside the box of carefully labeled thoughts and beliefs, and permission for yourself to discover something new.

I got to experience this feeling of free exploration during my honeymoon. For the longest time in my life, I thought that *my cards had been dealt* a certain way and that my destiny was written in stone after I became a wife and a mother. My life was no longer about **ME** and my choices; it was about my responsibilities to all my loved ones first. The responsibilities I had chosen for myself.

But the moment I allowed myself to play, my perspective on life opened a completely new chapter of possibility. During my time in Cambodia, I learned the art of getting oxygen into my lungs and simply being fully present in the moment. Unlike my daily life at home, where I felt perpetually *on guard,* in Cambodia I had the freedom to simply **BE**. I realized how much I loved freedom. Freedom to experience full joy in all moments.

The moment I allowed myself to dream bigger and make my dreams more vivid, I began to see life through a completely different lens of possibilities. My old life of perfectionism and chronic desire to *always be doing something* seemed like a distant memory. It was like it belonged to a completely different person, and I was only in the second week of my personal honeymoon.

When I returned to Kuala Lumpur, I felt as if I had accelerated at the speed of light, finally incorporating into my cells everything I had been learning and reading for years. I was now completely immersed in the energy of what **MORE** meant to **ME**. Something had definitely changed in my mind, in my relationship with my own beliefs. This transformation was also felt in the energy I projected to others.

Ajit Nawalkha, co-founder of Mindvalley, now my close friend and mentor, took me out to lunch to explore my path within the company and my vision for the future. What started as a casual conversation extended into two hours of one of the most profound and enriching conversations I ever had in my entire life. Ajit's genuine care and curiosity had always set him apart, and for the first time in as long as I could remember, I felt completely heard and seen. My story felt important and my vision was relevant to someone else. This lunch conversation was the catalyst for monumental transformative change within myself.

I had been designing my ideal life on paper for years and dreaming about it. However, this was the first opportunity to express it to another human being and vocalize my vision of creating a real impact in the world. That conversation brought my vision to life, making it feel more tangible and attainable. I could clearly see where I wanted to go and finally felt like I was on the way to living my destiny.

Ajit and I talked about everything. The rivers of thoughts and creative possibilities flowed from my heart with an ease that impressed me. My infinite capabilities became tangible, and I could feel the wings on my back vibrate sonorously as every word was waking them up from a very long slumber. I felt a powerful rush of adrenaline throughout my body as I allowed my soul to speak freely without limitations. We talked about our mission, about the legacy we wanted to leave the world, and ultimately discovered that our hearts were aimed at the same thing: creating a transformative impact on the world and supporting changemakers to create a ripple effect on others.

A few years earlier, Ajit had founded Mindvalley Coach, the coaching division of Mindvalley, and now wanted to expand it further. He wanted to enable people from all corners of the world to become better coaches, leaders, and most importantly, compassionate human beings. His goal was to empower people to support others in their communities, speaking in their own languages. All of this rooted in the values of love and service. This mission resonated so deeply in my soul that it made me want to cry with joy. That was a big *AHA* moment for me. I finally had a clear understanding of my purpose on Earth. For the first time, I was absolutely sure of my future.

I had found my calling in the world of coaching.

Ajit was looking for a learning experience designer for Mindvalley Coach, someone to help him co-create various educational programs that would help people develop their coaching skills and competencies through education to improve their lives and help others do the same. My inner nerd jumped for joy! The role was about learning and then teaching others, all aligned with a powerful mission. It was literally my dream role.

As the insatiable learner that I've always been, this was the perfect opportunity to use my passion for investigation and use it in service of others. I could see myself doing this for the rest of my life, working closer with people, helping them open their minds and flow with the same inspiration I was experiencing at that moment.

"I have no idea how to do everything you just said, but if you give me a month, I will learn how to do it," I told him.

Ajit smiled, knowing how close this was to my heart, and trusting fully that I would figure out what I needed for the role. That conversation pivoted my entire career and opened up a whole new world of opportunities for what would become the direction of my life. In that moment, I recognized the incredible power of having a person who truly cares about you believing in your potential. This breathes life into your wings and prepares you to fly.

I ended my month-long honeymoon with a completely different perspective on life, I became a pranic healer on my last weekend in Kuala Lumpur, I learned more about subtle energies, I opened my heart to give and receive, I incorporated more confidence into my being and learned to tune into divine guidance. It was an expansive and delicious experience for my soul!

Journal Insight Questions

One of the most transformative exercises I have ever used for myself and with my clients is called "The 3 Most Important Questions." This exercise was developed by Vishen Lakhiani, founder of Mindvalley, and it is aimed to change your entire perspective of life in just a few minutes. It will help you redefine the way you envision your future.

Imagine that you have unlimited resources (time, money, help, skills, etc), and you have complete certainty that you can do anything. What would you like your life to look and feel like in the next 3-5 years?

Take 5 minutes to make a quick list of what you want for each one of the next 3 categories (spend about 90 seconds per category). Just write the first thing that comes to your mind

*I know 90 seconds feels like a very short time, but this is intentional. It is designed to *turn off* your rational mind and activate your creative mind. When you finish your first list, then you can revisit what you wrote and expand it (or even create a vision board).

Use the guiding questions to get you started, then add your own ideas!

1. **Experiences:** This is what you want to experience as a human. It involves your emotions, your environment, the people that you want to share your time with, and what you want to explore.
   a. What do you want to experience in your life?
   b. Where do you want to travel?
   c. Who are you spending your life with? How is your home?
   d. How do you feel every day?
   e. How are your relationships?
   f. What hobbies are you exploring?

2. **Growth:** This is about the ways that you want to expand your knowledge, gain new skills, and develop new insights.
   a. What do you want to learn?
   b. What new skills do you want to develop?
   c. What character traits do you want to improve?
   d. How can you learn to take better care of yourself?
   e. What other areas of yourself do you want to develop?

3. **Contribution:** This is about what you want to give back to the world, your community, your family, and other things that are close to your heart.
   a. What is the legacy that you want to leave in the world?
   b. If you could solve one major problem for humanity, what would that be?
   c. How do you want to be remembered?
   d. What are some causes that you want to help?
   e. What movements do you want to start in your community / your country / the world?

This simple exercise will kickstart your imagination to a new holistic level, allowing you to gather more feathers on your journey of building your wings. Notice how much of what you want is already available for you and how easy it becomes to create your dream life one day at a time.

PART 3

REDEFINE YOUR "NEW NORMAL": CREATE YOUR UNIQUE WINGS

All of us have the power to steer our life in any direction that we want,
no matter where we are in our journey, or how long we
have been going in a certain direction. The ultimate
person in charge of where we want to go is *us*.

Life is always full of choices, no matter who you are, what you are
going through, or what happened in your past. Once you remember
that you have the power to choose your own destiny, you can begin to
make conscious decisions about each step you want to take forward.

It is about having the determination to fight for what you want
to create and trust that everything you need in your journey
will be available to you when you are ready to receive it.

This is about seeking the reason that your soul is on this
planet, connecting to your purpose, remembering that
everything happens *for* you, instead of *to* you,
and that you can shift your perspective to shift your reality.

This is how you can find the unique feathers
that will create your unique wings.

"Ninety-nine percent of all failures come from people who have a habit of making excuses."

– George Washington Carver

CHAPTER 10

PERSONAL RESPONSIBILITY

*O*nce you recognize that every human being has the innate ability to take control of their own life and that everyone has the same inner power as you, you free yourself from the enormous responsibility of trying to *fix the world*. Only then you can focus on the only thing that you are responsible for—YOUR life.

Taking ownership of your own life is where the real magic starts to happen within and around you. And just like you, everyone else is responsible for the choices they make for their own life experience. So release your self-imposed responsibility for others.

Think of this release as a way to give power back to the people you love. Let that sink in.

The more you take on other people's responsibilities, the less they can learn how to do things themselves. Consider these questions:

- If you make decisions for your loved ones, how will they learn to make a decision on their own?
- If you constantly take care of another person's chores, how will they learn to be self-sufficient?
- If you are always looking for ways to help those around you avoid any uncomfortable feelings, how will they learn to manage their own emotions?

And these are just a few examples of what we as *loving humans* tend to do. Thinking that love is taking care of the whole life operation of those whom we care for. Then we end up being resentful and feeling exhausted and we don't understand why!

The first thing you have to incorporate in your being is knowing that the world is not going to stop turning without you. There was a moment in human history when you didn't exist, and there will be another time in history when you will leave this planet. The people that you love will have to find their way with or without you.

The second thing to understand is that every time you want to take care of somebody else's challenges, all you are doing is robbing them of their personal power. You are taking away the opportunity to learn their own way of creating their life. In the end, a person without any personal responsibility is never going to be able to take care of themselves.

I am not saying that you stop caring for people. It is quite the opposite. Care so much that you allow others to fall so they learn how to get up on their own. Love others so much that you let them manage their own emotions so they can tackle anything that shows up in their lives. Believe in the people that you love so much, that you trust that they have the ability to figure things out on their own.

It is perfectly normal to take 24/7 care of a human when they are a defenseless baby or to be on constant vigilance when they are toddlers. What is not okay is when you continue this vigilant operation when the ones you love become adults (like you). So take a moment to reflect on your close relationships, and see how the responsibility balance is set. Also, remember that everything can be modified because you are the creator of your life.

When I left for my month in Kuala Lumpur, I was afraid of the millions of consequences that my absence could have brought to my loved ones. I was afraid of the terrible results that could come if I took time away from my everyday responsibilities to create space for myself. However, when I returned, I discovered that no one had died, no one had gone into depression, and nothing had broken. This was an incredible wake-up call from the Universe to help me change my Latina mom's *fix-it-all* mentality.

I asked the Universe to guide me so I could understand this new revelation more deeply. That led me to Ricardo Vilchez, a friend of my dad who specialized in regression therapy to be able to find in past lives some of the patterns that we currently have. My intention was clear: I wanted to understand, on a cellular level, how to free myself from my constant impulse to want to *fix* everyone's life. I needed to remember how it felt to be fully free of the self-imposed responsibility for other people's experiences.

Upon entering Ricardo's office, he gently guided me into a meditative state that allowed me to mentally travel to a moment in my past when I saw myself living a life where everything flowed naturally, and my only responsibility was my own experience. I closed my eyes and entered an altered state of consciousness. A vivid image came to mind. I was a 70-year-old man in the 15th century. A captain of a medium-sized wooden ship sailing the waters of South America. My body was lean, tanned, and muscular. I had long gray hair, which flowed freely in the wind as I sailed through the open sea.

In my visualization, I had lived much of my life as a nomad, taking my boat from coast to coast, where I would spend a few months at a time living with different tribes, absorbing their knowledge, sharing their foods and customs, and then passing on their stories to other tribes. I wasn't fixing anyone. I wasn't judging anyone. I was just a carrier of information and stories, creating connections between tribes as I ventured from coast to coast. I was an observer of life, a permanent learner, a simple human being who shared his existence with others. I lived an incredible life. I could remember the feeling of fullness in my heart from the simple fact of existing and the immense feeling of freedom that ran through my veins.

One day, aboard my ship, I felt it was time to leave the earthly plane. I didn't feel sadness or fear; I just knew in my heart that my time to die had come. A serene smile painted my lips knowing that I had lived a full life. I docked my boat on the shore and approached the leader of the tribe, giving all my worldly possessions to him and his people. We celebrated my transition through a ceremony of shared stories, fire, and food. Everyone was happy for me, and I felt a deep sense of serenity. When dawn broke, I ventured deep into the forest. There, I lay down on a bed of brown leaves under a large old tree, closed my eyes, and surrendered my body to the earth. I remember experiencing a lot of peace before I died, and then I just let myself go.

This profound experience helped me question my current reality: **What would happen if it no longer existed?**

Surely there would be a period of grieving, but eventually, each person in my life would find their way and take responsibility for their existence. So *why had I put so much pressure on myself to fix everything?* If I truly loved others as I said I did, I had to allow them to grow and experience life in the way their soul had chosen to experience it before incarnating on this planet. When I accepted the power to choose my own reality, I realized that every person has the same power, regardless of their age, economic situation, or cultural background. I knew I needed to share this enormous knowledge with the world, so I decided to become a Coach.

Journal Insight Questions

Reflect and Delegate

Take a moment to reflect on how you balance personal responsibility for yourself and your loved ones—your kids, your partner, your close friends and family, your clients.

- Write down all the things that you do for others. Things that you assume as your personal responsibility.
    - Write everything that comes to mind, from doing the chores at home, to emotionally taking care of them.
- From that list, identify the things that belong to someone else.
    - What are the things from the to-do list that you are currently doing for others, that you want to take off your plate because they are someone else's responsibility?
- Delegate!

With this clarity, and with the knowledge that life can change for anyone and this is okay, then you can have a conversation with your loved ones to start to delegate back their personal responsibility. Will you find resistance? I am pretty certain you will in a way because change is not easy. But your loved ones will deal with that change and grow because of it. ;)

CHAPTER 11

QUESTION
YOUR
"REALITY"

There is a concept that Vishen Lakhiani created in his book *The Code of the Extraordinary Mind* that blew my mind because it allowed me to shift the way I understood my reality. This concept is called **BRULES**, which stands for *"Bullshit Rules."*

BRULES are the societal norms, beliefs, and expectations that we often unquestioningly accept and follow without considering whether they align with our values, desires, or goals. Unfortunately, we see these rules as the absolute truth and rarely even question them, because we have repeated them for so long that they become part of our reality.

BRULES can limit our potential and hinder our ability to live authentically and passionately. The majority of these BRULES are created by the society in which we are born to help us have a simple understanding of the world, and they vary from one culture to another. BRULES are things like:

- You have to get married before you are 30, or you'll be forever alone.
- You should get married and have children if you want to live a full life.

- You need to get a college degree (or multiple degrees) if you want to be successful in life.
- If you want to make money, you have to hustle for the majority of your life.
- Money is hard to get.
- Men should be the financial provider of the home, and women must take care of the home and children.
- Some people just *get lucky*, the rest of us should suffer.

And like these, many BRULES have created the script that governs how you live, how you make decisions, how you feel, and how you show up in the world. But if you really think about it, there are only a few absolute truths that apply to all human beings (like: you will die someday), and the vast majority of the other rules can be questioned, especially those that don't serve the reality that you want to create. Letting go of the idea that what you know so far is an *absolute truth* is a liberating experience that allows you to see a completely new and different perspective of what life can BE.

When we are children, we tend to take everything the adults around us tell us as absolute truth. The way we are raised and the society in which we grow up builds the beliefs that shape who we are when we become adults. It is understandable that you blindly follow these beliefs as a kid, but there comes a point in your life when you have the right and responsibility to question what beliefs are serving you and what beliefs you are ready to let go of.

I never thought that I had permission to question the set of rules that I had been handed until I got the chance to experience a different reality in Kuala Lumpur. When I came home from my personal honeymoon, I felt like a completely different human being. As I hugged my children, I felt a different, more powerful kind of love. I savored their hugs and smiles, listened from presence, and enjoyed our moments without the shadow of my *to-do* list. I stopped doing things because *I had to*, and started doing things because *I chose to*. I discovered that I had become more transparent as the elaborate masks I had painstakingly constructed throughout my life had dissolved during the time I was away from home. I had granted myself the freedom to discover my true SELF.

I also noticed that I had lost connection with my husband. I realized that we had lived in the same house for years, but we lived completely different lives. Beyond discussing household chores, it was difficult to find common ground, and none of our life interests were aligned anymore. I'm sure he felt it too because every relationship is made or broken between two people. We had too many disagreements, we spent too much time apart, and everyone did their own thing. We had simply allowed ourselves to grow apart over the years.

This period of my life was full of changes in all areas of my life, and I couldn't face them all at once, nor did I want to. I had learned to ask for Divine guidance, and that is precisely what I did. The answer was to take things slow and focus on making changes in ONE area of my life at a time, starting with my career. I quit my second job at the real estate development company I had worked at for seven years. While I appreciated the experience, I recognized that it was no longer aligned with my future vision. I also transitioned my customer service team to another leader and immersed myself in the new world of coaching and creating learning experiences.

My transformation had a ripple effect on my children. We all began to question our current reality and learned to listen to our heart's desires instead of society's expectations. We evolved as a family, as individuals, as souls embarking on the journey of life. I reduced my son's therapies to introduce more fun into his life. It was clear that he was ready to face life more independently and prepare for college. Eduardo graduated from high school and, instead of pursuing a conventional career, followed his passion for studying video game design and voice-over acting. His enthusiasm for fictional characters was boundless, and he flourished in the realm of self-exploration.

I stopped being the *dancer mom* who spent countless hours in rehearsals and competitions when my daughter changed her focus to dancing for the sheer love of it, rather than living solely to dance. Avi embraced dance as a source of joy, free from the constraints of competition. She learned to love her unique form of expression as she entered her teenage years, with her concerns shifting away to make room for passion, igniting her inner fire.

My husband, however, continued as he always did, staying the same, working as an incredible veterinary doctor, but allowing the worries and responsibilities of day-to-day life to take over his reality. He was seeking to escape reality instead of embracing change, and he was also struggling to accept the changes that were happening within me. The tangled web of responsibilities I had carefully piled on my shoulders was dissolving, and I was no longer willing to handle everything alone. I wanted to help my husband. Part of me wanted to *save him* and *fix everything,* but another part of me knew I had to let go of the urge to live other people's lives and let things go their own way.

This was a lesson that my friend, the late Psalm Isadora, taught me during an immersive personal development retreat called Afest, here in Costa Rica. She taught others to use sensuality and the power of connecting with that energy to regain personal power. After her session, she invited me to a workshop she was teaching that same night. I was immediately scared because it meant investing a significant sum of money and also leaving my comfort zone, so I began to explain all the difficult things in my life that made it impossible for me to attend her workshop.

She stopped looking at me, put her hands inside her purse, and started searching for something. I watched her curiously, wondering what she was doing. After a few moments, she looked at me with a very serious face and said:

"I couldn't find any."
"Find any what?" I asked
"Fucks!" She blurted as she threw her hands into the air. "I am all out of fucks, so I have ZERO fucks to give."

I was frozen by the comment at the time. It was only later that I was able to fully understand the meaning behind her words. I realized that I had always been so focused on my situation and the *victim* role that I had created for myself, that I couldn't see past it. I also realized that much of the weight I had carried throughout my life had been self-imposed by labeling everything based on how other people saw the world, with words that simply didn't let me see beyond my own limitations.

For the first time in my life, I grabbed my constricting inner *label maker,* threw it in the trash, and added a new label maker to my vocabulary. One full of new ideas that I wanted to incorporate into my life and leave room to question my reality. I also embraced the power of letting go of what other people thought was best for me, giving myself space to choose for ME.

Looking back at my life with grace, I realized that I always did the best I could with the available resources I had at the time. And I understood that I had the power to choose the experiences I wanted to shape my future. That realization led me to finding so many wonderful feathers to build my wings.

Journal Insight Questions

- Make a list of the current rules that you hold in different areas of your life. The areas that you described in Chapter 7 (*"What do you want?"*): Your health, Emotional life, Spirituality, Family, Love relationship, Social life, Intellect, and Finances.
    - o Represent each of these categories with a feather of a different color (so you notice where the majority of your rules lie).
- Notice the rules that apply to you now based on your conscious decisions, and then notice which of them are brules.
    - o Remember, the BRULES are the *"rules of life"* that you learned at some point in your life, but that no longer serve you, or are not aligned to your current beliefs.
- For the rules that you want to keep, briefly reflect on why you chose to keep them.
- For the BRULES that you want to let go of, write the new rule or belief that you want to incorporate instead, along with one thing that you can do to reinforce these new beliefs.
- Now notice the different colors of your feathers, and feel the new energy that comes from them thanks to your new rules of life.

"The two most important days in life are the day you born and the day you find out why."

– Mark Twain

CHAPTER 12

FIND YOUR PURPOSE

There is nothing more exciting than knowing the reason why you came to this planet. Nothing is better than discovering what makes your heart sing and makes you jump out of bed in the morning. Having a clear purpose drives every area of your being and makes every moment of your existence feel complete. Finding your life purpose is a search that can only be led by your heart and makes everything else worthwhile.

I know this sounds magical and that is because it IS. It is a force that moves you from the inside out, a light that shines on everything you do and gives you meaning. But how do you find your purpose in *real life*? Elizabeth Gilbert, best-selling author of *Eat, Pray, Love*, simply explains this, in one of her YouTube videos, where she talks about the distinction between Hobbies, Jobs, Careers, & Vocation.

A Hobby is a great way for you to connect to something you love. There is no need for you to do it, but you choose to do it anyway because it brings you joy. It may or may not be connected to your profession, and it typically won't bring you money (although some hobbies do).

A Job is a means for you to fulfill your Earthly needs (pay the bills). It is something that you do with a specific goal in mind, which is to get money. This is a way for you to become independent and take care of your needs so you don't place that responsibility on others. A job is also *not* your life. It may align or not with your passions or interests; it is just something you *do*. It's perfectly okay to have a job while you are looking for your vocation. You are a human after all, and live in a world with human needs.

A Career is a job that you are *passionate* about. Something that you do that is in line with your core values, where you want to develop and learn more because you *choose* to. This is something that you *love* to do, something you look forward to, and something that you are constantly looking to give more of your time and energy to because you are committed.

A Vocation is your *Divine Calling*, an invitation from the Universe to express your unique gifts to the world through an occupation or profession. Something that you do based on your skills, interests, and values. It has a deeper *meaning* than a career, makes you feel fulfilled, and creates an impact on others.

Then you have **Purpose**. Simon Sinek, best-selling author of *Start with Why* talks about **purpose** as the fundamental reason for your existence that is aligned with your core values. It guides your actions and decisions and encompasses a deeper sense of meaning, fulfillment, and direction in life beyond just achieving specific goals or outcomes.

The main difference between a Vocation and a Purpose is that a Vocation is something that you **DO**, while a Purpose is who you **ARE**. While they may overlap for some people, they serve different roles in shaping your identity, values, and sense of fulfillment.

My personal journey led me to the field of coaching. I could see the profound impact that genuine presence and authentic connections with oneself and others can have on the evolution of humanity. Coaching encompassed all the parts that had built my life. It linked all the highs, the lows, the times I fell and got back up, all the times I found magic in the world, as well as those where I found disappointment. The moments when I found peace in stillness and the moments when I wanted to jump for joy. All these experiences opened a new world for me to explore through coaching.

When you are in the middle of adolescence, you are expected to find a professional career that is connected to your deepest essence and to have clarity about what you want to do with the rest of your life by the time you graduate from school, which in my case was at the tender age of 17.

The truth is, I had no idea what I wanted to do for the rest of my life at 17! The options seemed too limited at the time in my country: You could become a lawyer, a doctor, an engineer, or study business administration. Any other career choice seemed to condemn you to a life of financial hardship.

The issue was that I wasn't only ONE thing. I was a collection of interests, a multi-passionate woman who was curious to explore different areas of life, from the arts to different approaches to science. When I went to school, I chose Business Administration based solely on the fact that I didn't know what else to do, not because it was my passion.

My entire world changed when I discovered the world of personal growth. I immersed myself in the power of questioning *reality* and remembered that we are here to live a full life. That life-changing conversation with Ajit during my first journey of self-discovery had such immense power that it allowed me to clearly see the power of coaching in action.

I had found my calling!

Coaching is not about leaving your past behind. Rather, it is about accepting every part of yourself as an ecosystem designed to help you and others live the best version of themselves. It incorporates all your interests, all your passions, all your life lessons, and all of who **YOU** are. In this profession, you have to be constantly learning, you have to become a curious explorer of life, and be ready to celebrate the beautiful tapestry of your existence, bound by the threads of what makes you human. Coaching allows you to connect with others in a deeper and more meaningful way, daring them to reclaim their inner power so they remember that they can design their reality on their terms.

After I transitioned to coaching, my life became my playground of personal exploration, and I learned to receive each experience with an open heart. I reconnected with all my stories, I reconciled with my flaws, I released the past that no longer served me, I was grateful for the situations that helped me grow, and I propelled myself forward with a new direction focused on purpose. I finally understood the true essence of *purpose.*

Doing something you are passionate about not only affects the way you think about things but also makes you feel alive in every cell of your body. Embodying your purpose means that everything you do is infused with the powerful energy of your heart and guided by your soul. It is about loving all of your feathers, no matter how they look like; because all of them are important parts of your wings.

I wanted more of *that.*

Journal Insight Questions

There are many exercises out there that will guide you to find your purpose. I am going to share the one that helped me the most because of its simplicity - based on just five questions.

Even though the questions are simple, allow yourself time to really think about them as they will create your own unique blueprint of your purpose. This blueprint will be the way that you put your feathers together when you build your wings.

And don't wait until you have everything figured out before you start to do what brings you joy and fulfillment. You can do this any-where, in any job you have, or in any life situation you are in. Just set the intention, and the rest will come to you.

Question 1. Who Are You?

Apart from the external labels that society knows about you, who are you really?

- What are your core values?
- What are your main beliefs about life?
- What are your strengths and weaknesses?
- What is most important for you in this life?
- What makes you feel alive?
- What does success mean for you?

Question 2. Who do you serve?

These are the people that you want to impact in the world.

- Who is the ideal person that you feel most called to help?
- Who are the types of people that you feel excited to talk to?
- What are they doing in the world?
- What do they want?
- What is their biggest dream?
- What is their greatest challenge?
- What keeps them up at night?
- What do they need to achieve their dream life?

Question #3. How do you serve?
This is how you serve the world by using your gifts.

- What are your biggest skills?
- Why do people come to you for help?
- What is that thing that you can't stop talking about?
- What are you most interested in learning all the time?
- What makes you lose track of time?
- What is something that you would do even if you didn't get paid for it?

Question 4. What results do you create?
This is the way that you create an impact in the world and bring value.

- How do you help the people you work with to get closer to their goals and dreams?
- What is the pain that you are helping them solve?
- What challenges can people overcome after working with you?
- What is something unique that you bring to people?
- How do people feel after working with you?
- How do the people who work with you think differently? Get a different perspective?
- What do people compliment you the most on?

Question 5. How can you make living your purpose sustainable?
This is how you make sure that all your needs are met so you can pursue your purpose for a long time.

If you know who you are, what you do best, who you do it for, and what results you bring, are you able to get paid for this? If not yet, it's okay, you can define another source of income in the meantime. Just make sure you know how much you need to cover your needs and start to build your offer with the questions below.

If you are getting paid to pursue your calling:

- What is your current offer to the world?
- What other ways do you have where you can create an impact on the people you serve? Consider creating books, retreats, workshops, new products, etc.
- What are some of the mediums you use to talk about what you do with the world? (Social media, podcast, YouTube, etc)
- What are some innovative ways to serve that you want to explore?

CHAPTER 13

SET BOUNDARIES

*H*ave you ever felt like you give too much to others but they don't *notice?* Have you ever felt resentful of your loved ones because you are expecting them to give you what you give to them? (Or at least be grateful). Have you ever gone into burnout? Have you ever reached a point in your life where you just feel like you want to go to a distant mountain and be by yourself?

On the other hand, have you ever gone to somebody's house and suggested they change something without them asking for it? Have you ever given unsolicited advice to a friend because you felt like you knew what was best for them? Have you ever taken over someone else's responsibility because you think that you can *do it better*?

If you answered yes to one or more of these questions, you may have some trouble setting boundaries for yourself or respecting other people's boundaries. And don't feel bad; you are not alone in this! I had zero boundaries, and I'm still working on this myself.

At some point in our lives, we get programmed with this BRULE that boundaries are a *bad thing* that can be limiting. But boundaries are not a way to limit your relationships. They are rather one of the most important ways that exist for you to be able to maintain healthy relationships, promote self-care, and protect your well-being. And if you want to live an extraordinary life, you are going to want to have the most abundant energy to be able to create from an unlimited place.

Imagine your boundaries as the *protective guard rails* of your energy, where you get to decide what situations you allow to come in, and what situations should stay away from you. These can be set based on your wants and needs, even if you never set them before.

My friend and coach Carlos Nuñez delivers a powerful seminar on this exact topic called Fronteras (Borders). He talks about boundaries like the borders that divide the countries. These are imaginary lines that were created based on agreements from the countries to guard the integrity of each region, control who comes in or out, allow each country to create its own laws, and decide the way its inhabitants want to live their lives.

In the same way that countries can create borders based on agreements, you can create borders of your own to protect your energy and protect the energy of the people around you. Boundaries serve both parties *always*, and they are meant to cultivate healthy relationships that can be sustainable over time.

Let me tell you my story about setting boundaries. I grew up in Costa Rica during a time when our society was still largely dominated by masculine energy. Even though my mom was an incredibly strong role model of womanhood, her parenting approach was still guided by the scripts incorporated by the male population. I have two older brothers, and I remember that they were treated very differently than I was. While it was normal for me as a woman to cook, serve, and help clean the house, for my brothers it was normal to be taken care of. My brothers were encouraged to go out and enjoy themselves, while I was asked to be careful about having *too much fun* to prevent others from talking. Guilt was incorporated from childhood as a way to model young women into complacent adults.

Despite my brothers' unconditional love and protective nature, there were times when I felt like a fragile porcelain doll. Someone who needed to be *rescued,* and that made me angry! I constantly fought against this different treatment we received based solely on our genitals. I struggled with being judged and having different expectations simply for being a woman.

However, as I grew older, I slowly and unconsciously incorporated the *people pleaser / "perfect woman"* beliefs into my daily life. I learned to cook, sew, and even took quilting courses and many other crafts.

Although I graduated with a degree in Business Administration in college, a part of me had already resigned myself to the idea that my professional career would be secondary to my future role as *someone's wife*. A part of me had accepted the belief that to create wealth and security, I had to marry a powerful man, and that my role would be to support him as a devoted wife and mother. I believed that everything related to taking care of my home and my children was my exclusive responsibility, and I felt incredibly guilty when I didn't give it my all.

But after my personal honeymoon, everything changed. It was clear to me that my mother had passed on to me what she had learned, but that was not MY absolute truth. I knew I had to let go of my past limitations and learn to set healthy boundaries for myself so that I would not repeat the same patterns with my kids.

Everything in my *house operation* had been my sole responsibility during my entire marriage. My husband was the main financial provider, but I took care of everything else, from the grocery shopping to the caregiving and education of our kids—on top of my two jobs. I felt so drained at the end of my days that all I wanted to do was lock myself up in the bathroom to get a moment of peace and quiet. My bathroom was the only place in my home where both my kids and my husband respected my time alone, and this became my *boundary fortress* when I needed to escape life for a while.

For the longest time of my life, I felt like my role as a woman, mother, and wife was to be *on call* all my waking hours, but I ended up resenting everyone I loved for it. In the end, it wasn't their fault. They never asked for me to take care of everything. I had been the one who had set up an impossible operation, and they just grew accustomed to it.

I was ready to make a change. I NEEDED to make a change and I knew it, but I had no idea of where to start or how to do it, so I went to my room and turned on the TV to think about something else for a while. As I sat down on my bed, an old movie called The *Stepford Wives* starring Nicole Kidman was starting to play. It showed the life of a successful woman from New York, who decides to move to the Connecticut suburb of Stepford with her husband and kids to escape the hectic life of the city and be able to live in a more peaceful environment. They show you a *perfect* town with *perfect* women who are always dressed up impeccably as they tend to their husband's every need.

You see them cleaning their home with a big smile, while their husbands go out to work. Then receiving them at night with a drink, so they can relax on the couch while they cook. Then, the women served the *perfect* meal for their men. All of the little hairs in my arms rose with this movie. And don't get me wrong, I love preparing meals and taking care of my family, but this was different. It was too fake. Too pushed. Too perfect. But only for one person in the relationship. Everything was set up for the men in the community, while the women were *people-pleasing robots* that dedicated their entire energy to complying with their partners' needs.

That movie hit me hard because I saw myself in it. I had lived with the script in my head that when something could cause discomfort to another person, the best way for me to respond was to just *shut up and smile*. I believed for a long time that was my role. I just didn't want to be *a bother*.

But that built-up image that I had created for myself was no longer true for me. It wasn't a script that I wanted to run in my life. So after the movie ended, I sat down to write my new rules. The boundaries that I wanted to create for my life. I made a list of the things that made me feel expansive and the things that made me feel contracted. I got clear on the things that needed to change in my life so I could also enjoy the same nurturing and attention that I freely gave to everyone else.

That was the moment I learned to say **NO**. Those two magical letters had a very deep meaning for my new reality as they held the key to removing things from my plate that no longer aligned with what I wanted to do and made room for what really mattered to me. The magical **NO** built my boundaries and reminded me that everyone has the power to create their own reality (including me). It liberated me from guilt and my sense of obligation, inviting me to deepen my connection to my purpose.

This process helped free me from my chains, vowing to never again let my past decisions or conditioning define my future. I was finally able to shed the last layers of my programming, let go of the *perfect woman* disguise I had worn for so long, and I was able to tell the part of me that only lived to please others to go fuck itself. I realized that prioritizing myself didn't mean I was selfish; it actually meant I finally loved myself as strongly as I loved those around me.

This experience freed up the spaces between my feathers so they could move again, preparing me to fly.

Journal Insight Questions and Action Steps

In setting Boundaries, there are two parts that we are going to work on. The first one is about what you want and why that matters. Then the second one is in the way that you are going to communicate your boundaries to your loved ones.

Part 1. Get clarity on your boundaries

*You can go back to Chapter 10 ("Personal Responsibility") to remember the things that you want to get off your plate to balance the responsibility load from your important relationships.

- *Define Your Borders*: Think about the behaviors, actions, or situations that make you feel uncomfortable, stressed, or overstepped in your important relationships, and write them down in a list.
- *List Your Boundaries*: Write down a list of boundaries that you want to establish in different areas of your life. Be specific about what behaviors or actions are acceptable and unacceptable to you.
- *Set Consequences*: Be clear on the consequences for others disrespecting your boundaries.

Part 2. Communicate your boundaries

- *Set the tone:* Make sure you set time apart for having the important boundary conversation where the people you love are ready and open to listen without any distractions.
- *Communicate your boundaries:* Make sure your loved ones understand where you're coming from, why you decided to set the boundaries, and why they are important to you.

- **Listen:** In any relationship, you have to be open to sharing and listening. Make sure you also ask your loved ones to think about their own boundaries so you can all share.
- **Follow-up:** Book a follow-up conversation where everyone involved in the relationship can participate and share their boundaries. You can also discuss the consequences of trespassing the boundaries here as well.

CHAPTER 14

SHIFT YOUR FOCUS

I remember how curious I was as a child and how much I loved exploring outside. We didn't have access to all of these new technological gadgets at that time I was growing up, so we had to be creative. One of the things I remember that I found interesting was taking a magnifying glass out on a sunny day and trying to focus the energy of the sun through the lens to create heat. I was fascinated watching the small ray of light burn the leaves if I let it long enough. I was able to bring all the energy of the sun into a tiny object to create a magnified effect of the light and heat that it provides regularly.

This is *focus*.

The same happens with our thoughts. What we focus our attention on always tends to grow. If you focus your energy on the situations in your life that have brought you pain and suffering, you will create more pain and suffering. But when you shift your attention to what is going well in your life and the expansive energy of your dreams, suddenly limitations dissolve and you gain access to creation from a boundless place of infinite possibilities.

You see the world through your own lens, your own perspective that is guided by the beliefs that you hold and the stories you repeat to yourself. But you have the power to *change your perspective* anytime. Shifting your focus is like trying on a new pair of glasses that will help you see a different world so that no matter what happens outside of yourself, you can always choose how you want to respond. What you want to bring focus to.

Think about when you take a trip to a place you have never visited. You will look at your surroundings with curiosity and awe. That in turn makes you feel expansive and open. This is exactly why we travel and take vacations! Now imagine yourself going through your same daily routine. You are in traffic watching the same scenery as you do every single day, and you probably disassociate from it because you already know it. You focus on the next task ahead and then the following *to-do*. How does that make you feel?

Believe me, I really dislike traffic, especially living in Costa Rica. But that is a story for another day. The point here is that if you **change your focus**, that changes your **perspective**, which in turn changes your **experience**.

I learned how to shift my focus along my transformation journey. After learning how to set boundaries and be more selective with my energy, I was able to reclaim the space I had once freely given to the needs and desires of others before my own. I found myself overflowing with newfound inspiration and knew it was time to focus on empowering my dreams and aspirations. I was focused on what I wanted to create from that new openness inside of me, ready to receive the gifts that the Universe had in store for me.

I noticed how all of the areas of my life felt like they were upgrading slowly but steadily, except in my relationship with my husband. It felt like we were going in two very different directions. I was ready to fly, and he didn't even remember he had wings. But I stuck with our marriage and kept trying, for the sake of the family we had built together.

Mindvalley invited me to return to Kuala Lumpur for another month. It had been a year since my first visit, and this return was an exciting invitation to *come home to me*. There was a lot to tell, a lot of people to see, and a lot of new experiences to have. I could not wait! On this second trip to Asia, I decided to visit Bali.

I had pasted on my life vision board a long time ago the image of a Balinese temple in the middle of a lake. Something was calling me to visit it. I don't know if it was the tranquility that emanated from the photo of the wooden temple sitting peacefully in the middle of a majestic lake, but somehow, I knew there was a message there for me, and I had to find out what it was.

My friend Ericka, who had taught me to let go of fear the year before, came with me on that trip. When we arrived at Bandara International Airport Denpasar, the first thing we did was exchange 100 dollars into the local currency. When we received the handful of bills, we realized that this was equivalent to 1.5 million Indonesian Rupiahs. We had never had millions in our hands before, so we got to our hotel, threw the bills on our bed, and lay down on the pile of cash, laughing out loud.

"We are millionaires now!" we said in unison.

I knew the actual amount of money exchanged was only a hundred dollars, but it was the energy surrounding that moment that sparked something different within me. I looked around at the beautiful place we were staying and couldn't help but feel an overwhelming sense of abundance and expansion. It was very different from what I had been experiencing at home, and it served as a much-needed reminder to change my focus.

Our hotel was an old Balinese resort that had six small cabins surrounding an open terrace with a lovely place to eat in the corner. I was curious about the meaning of the open terrace, so I followed the elderly owner of the hotel, who was decorating it with baskets containing a variety of colorful offerings. She explained to me that the Balinese people made daily offerings to the spirits, seeking protection and blessings. These baskets, known as *Canang Sari,* were woven from palm leaves and filled with flowers, rice, and other small items, including incense and fruits, as an expression of gratitude to the Sang Hyang Widhi Wasa.

It suddenly became clear to me why the Balinese people radiated so much happiness: They practiced **gratitude** every day! They were grateful for everything: for waking up healthy, for the food they had, for the bright blue sky and the energy of life itself. It was a beautiful way to *focus* on the energy of **expansion**.

Ericka and I met for breakfast in the hotel's common area, eager to embark on the first tour we could find, hungry to explore the wonders of Bali. We booked the first thing we saw without knowing where it was going to take us. Then got on a small blue bus and began the tour. Our journey took us through lush green forests, filled with trees, banana groves, and rice terraces, and finally brought us to Lake Bratan.

When I got off the bus and approached the lake, my heart jumped out of my chest. I saw the temple I had on my life vision board! It was there, in the middle of the lake!

The Ulun Danu Bratan temple looked as amazing as the photo that adorned my life vision board at home, only in real life it was a much tinier version of what I had imagined. Ericka and I rented a small swan-shaped pedal boat and began our journey across the lake to reach the temple. We were quite the comedy movie: two grown women, sitting inside a swan-shaped boat, pedaling with all their might, but moving as slowly as a turtle on Valium. After an hour of superhuman effort and enduring an unexpected storm in the middle of our journey, we finally reached the temple.

We couldn't get off the boat to go inside because it was too small of a structure that was meant to be a symbolic decoration, so we pedaled around it. And then I realized something important. We often rush to reach a destination, expecting a great gift when we reach the goal. However, the real gifts are often discovered during the journey itself. All you have to do is bring your focus to those moments on the journey.

I thanked the Universe for my life and all the gifts I was receiving and headed back to the shore. At that moment, I realized it was time to come home to myself. I realized that after everything that had happened, the time had finally come to say YES to ME and make the decision that took me so many years to make. It was at that precise moment that I realized that the relationship with my husband had come to an end, and it was time for us to part ways.

Journal Insight Questions

Now that you have more clarity on the life that you want for yourself, I invite you to notice where you are focusing your attention. If you set an intention to find more feathers in every situation, you will find it easier to build your wings.

Reflect on your daily routine as it is right now in the context of the life that you want to lead:

- Is where you are focusing your energy serving your Higher Self?

- Are you focusing on activities that make you feel expansive or contractive?
- How can you shift your focus from situations that feel contractive?
- How are you purposefully looking for your own unique feathers?

"Healing may not be so much about getting better, as about letting go of everything that isn't you – all of the expectations, all of the beliefs – and becoming who you are."

– Rachel Naomi Remen

PART 4

HEALING

Healing is a journey of letting go of what no longer serves
you. This is about removing the layers of dust and rubble that
you have piled on top of your wings throughout the years
so they finally have enough space to move.

Healing has the immense power to reclaim
your energy to create something new.

Something magical that you forgot is available for you,
hiding beneath the pain and the fear, waiting to be revealed.

It frees you from the shackles that hold you to the ground.
Shackles which can be opened when you decide to forgive yourself,
so you can claim the power to fly on your own.

And before you can soar into the immensity of creation,
you have to release the heaviness of the past that no longer serves you.

"Let go of something old that no longer serves you in order to make room for something new."

– Roy T. Bennett

CHAPTER 15

RELEASE WHAT NO LONGER SERVES YOU

*H*ave you ever seen the television show *Hoarders*? That show gives you a glimpse into the lives of people who have a compulsion to accumulate tons of things over the years. In this show, you watch the slow deterioration of their environment as they accumulate layer after layer of things they keep buying compulsively until their home becomes their personal prison.

Once they are completely drowned under useless piles of things, you see a group of wonderful humans that jump in, wanting to help. You also see the struggle of the person with the hoarding problem when they are asked to release their *precious treasures*. Every bit of release is a personal battle as they grew accustomed to piling their pieces of safety through the years, even when the objects that they hold dear are the same ones preventing them from being free.

The same thing happens when you accumulate things that don't serve you anymore. Clinging to the memories of situations that already passed, holding to the heavy emotions that cut the oxygen from your life, and repeating the patterns that you don't want to release. Like a sad movie on a loop that makes you feel more miserable or angry every time you relive the same situations.

This is exactly why the act of releasing is so important when you want to create something new in your life. You have to make space for what you want to create for yourself before you can invite new energies into your life. This process is always about *your personal choice* to let go of the unnecessary weight that you carry so that you can be *free*.

Having the opportunity to choose your own destiny is an incredible gift, but it also comes with a deep responsibility. I was fully aware that I had to make some hard decisions that would affect not only myself but my husband and children as well. I needed to find the courage to untangle the gigantic knot in my throat that was preventing me from having the difficult conversation of ending my marriage of 17 years. Before I could do this, I knew I had to find the source of my problem, so I embarked on a journey to heal my inner child.

My parents divorced when I was 4 years old, and I have vivid memories of my dad's presence during my childhood that always made me feel safe, heard, and seen. But when they separated, it felt like a part of him abandoned me too. I felt abandoned when he started a new family, and I lost my special place in his heart. Although I now know this wasn't true, that's how I felt when I was little. A part of me still carried the scars of abandonment that led me to be a people pleaser when I became an adult to prevent people from leaving me.

My adult *self* could rationally understand that we are all imperfect human beings who make mistakes, but my inner child couldn't understand it. I recognized that I needed to create space for healing if I wanted to move forward.

During the Inner Child Healing therapy I experienced one of the most powerful meditations of my life. The guide took me back to a time in my childhood when I had made a subconscious pact to convince myself that I wasn't *good enough* and that my voice was not important. To the same moment I had told myself I had to make an extra effort to please others so they wouldn't abandon me. I saw myself when I was 4 years old. A happy girl full of freckles and blonde hair. I was running barefoot around our backyard, having complete confidence that the world had my back and that I was loved unconditionally.

But then I was transported to a day in December, just before Christmas. I walked into our house to find a large Christmas tree surrounded by brightly wrapped presents. I was so excited! I walked up to the tree and asked my mom if I could open one of mine. She smiled at me as she nodded. I launched myself towards a large red box decorated with a yellow bow that seemed gigantic to me. Just as I started to unwrap the gift, my dad walked in, clearly upset about something. He snatched the gift from me before I could finish opening it.

"These gifts should be opened on Christmas Day, not today," he scolded me.

I remember the pain I felt at that moment. Not just because my dad had taken the gift from me, but because he had raised his voice at me. I didn't understand that at that time, my parents were going through their own difficult process of breaking their relationship and that none of their external frustration and fighting was ever about me. My inner child thought that she had to be *a good little girl* to deserve to be loved and not be abandoned. I made a contract with myself at 4 years old to learn to *be quiet and smile* so as not to cause any problems. I came to understand how the contract this 4-year-old had made had quietly influenced my decisions as an adult, and I was ready to let it go.

In my mind, I traveled back in time to embrace my inner child, snuggling her in my arms and reassuring her that she would always be loved. I told her how much she mattered and that she would always be protected. Then I was able to free the knot from her throat so she could be free to speak her heart, knowing she had a right to speak her truth always.

After that experience, I sat down with my father to talk about what happened in the early years of my life. He opened up about his fears, as a man who was working hard to sustain his family, and didn't have the tools to manage the stress of his responsibilities at that age. He had never been taught to manage his own emotions as a kid himself. He also had to repress his voice from the outer world. We talked for hours. Not as a father and daughter, but as human to human, understanding that we all have a story behind who we become, but that doesn't define who we are going to be. I forgave him wholeheartedly, we hugged and cried together, releasing any glimpse of pain or hurt from the past. My dad and I are really close today. He is an amazing father and grandfather, and he has also helped me heal my own mistakes with raising my kids, by reminding me to forgive myself with grace.

This transformative experience helped me heal many wounded aspects of myself. It allowed me to see my parents from a different perspective. I could understand them as a mother myself, knowing in my heart that no one comes to this Earth with the purpose of hurting others. I now understand that at some point in our lives, something can break us and we just try to do the best we can with the situation. We can choose to hold on to that pain and let it fester inside us, or we can choose to let it go and be free. And just like when you release a helium balloon into the sky, I let go of the pent-up pain, resentment, and feelings of lack that I had stored up for years. Then I watched as they dissolved into the vastness of the sky, becoming smaller and smaller over time.

The week after the conversation with my father, I embarked on a hike with a Quero shaman to the lagoon of the Barva volcano in Costa Rica, looking to let go of the final parts of me that felt the guilt and pain of ending my marriage. The shaman asked us to choose three stones and put within them everything we wanted to release from our life experiences. We walked in silence for hours, each step carrying the weight of our stones and the burdens we wanted to release. I intentionally put in each stone the situations that I wanted to leave in the past. The fights, the hurt, and the resentment were deeply ingrained in my stones.

When we arrived at the lake, the shaman performed a small ceremony, expressing gratitude for the experiences of our lives and the energy we were willing to release contained within the stones, recognizing the lessons that each situation had left us. Finally, we were asked to throw our stones into the water so that they could be released from our reality and transmuted into the new energy we wanted to embody for ourselves.

After that day, I no longer carried the weight of the pain on my shoulders. I was ready to speak from my heart. I decided that my past would not define my future. I was ready to start over with a clean slate, and that the decisions I would make for myself would be based only on possibilities. I WAS FREE.

Action Steps

I will share with you two releasing practices that have worked best for me and my clients throughout the years. These are two simple ways for you to let go of anything that is no longer in alignment with who you are, or what you want to create for your life.

You can try only one of them or both. Feel what works best for you! You can also repeat these practices with different emotions, stories, beliefs, or patterns that you want to release. As many times as you need to feel like you are no longer attached to what you want to let go of.

1. *The Egg Practice*

When you have a heavy emotion that you don't know how to manage (like fear or anger for example), and you want to physically feel the release, this technique is fantastic.

- Go outside to a place where you can have a space for yourself to emote freely.
- Hold an egg with both hands and imagine you are putting everything you want to release inside of it.
- Physically feel how everything you want to release is somehow transferring from your mind and your heart into the tiny egg. Fill the egg completely.
- Once you feel like everything you want to let go is inside of the egg, and you no longer feel it in your body, grab the egg with one hand and destroy it
  - o You can smash it against something or step on it. Anything that physically destroys the egg.
- Notice how you feel in your body after you do this. Breathe that in.

*You can repeat this process as many times as you need. I have had days where I have used a full dozen!

2. *The Release Letter*

This is a great technique when you want to release a story, a belief, or a pattern that you haven't been able to let go of.

- Find a calm place where you can spend at least 30 minutes undisturbed so you can be with your thoughts.
- Take a deep breath. Give yourself permission to feel what you have to feel, and allow any thought that needs to show up to do so without judgment.
- Take a piece of paper and a pen (not a notebook or journal, but rather something you can destroy after), and write down what you want to release from your life.
- Go into as much detail as possible, describe everything that no longer serves you, allowing yourself to release the weight of this energy in the paper.
- Once you feel that you have emptied in the paper everything you are ready to let go, grab it in your hands, and crumple the paper into a ball. Then burn it (in a safe place of course).
- Observe as the paper is reduced to ashes, taking what you want to release with it. Then take the ashes and flush them down the toilet or into the wind.
- Feel the liberation in your mind and body, and breathe that in.

You can also repeat this process as many times as you need. The idea of these practices is to help you clear what you no longer want to hold in your life. This release takes away the heaviness from your wings so nothing can hold you to the ground when you are ready to take flight.

CHAPTER 16

FORGIVE

$\mathcal{F}$orgiveness is a transformative process that enriches your life, fostering inner peace, emotional well-being, and compassion toward yourself and others. It liberates you from the burden of pain, allowing you to feel lighter and more resilient. Moreover, forgiveness positively impacts your overall health by reducing stress and strengthening your immune system. By embracing forgiveness, you break free from the cycle of hurt and dismantle patterns of thoughts and emotions that disrupt your inner peace.

Forgiveness is a journey of self-discovery and empowerment. Everything related to forgiveness revolves around YOU, *your* healing, and *your* growth. You have the power to release what no longer serves you, regardless of whether the other person chooses to forgive you or not. It's not about erasing the past, but rather *reclaiming your power* in the present, and shaping your future without being defined by past experiences.

We all have a story of how we came to be who we are. A collection of moments and situations that slowly added layers on top of layers of how we navigate our relationships with others based on the lens of our own experience. I believe that no one's life dream as a kid is to become an asshole when they grow up. Nobody wishes to hurt other people or to cause pain. I also believe that everyone is always doing the best they can with the resources that they have available at the time.

When you can recognize the humanity behind the person who hurt you and try to see the world from their eyes, you will understand that hurt people tend to hurt others. This doesn't mean that you have to allow yourself to get hurt just because the other person suffered. It means that you have the power to *free* yourself from the pain, situation, and person who hurt you. You always have a *choice* about your personal experience moving forward.

I am going to share with you how forgiveness allowed me to make the best out of a very difficult situation. I had been ignoring the gap that had taken 10 years to build between my husband and me, carefully placing my emotions under a heavy interior rug so they wouldn't haunt me. I did this so I could continue to hold on to the family I had fought so hard to create. I wanted to give my children a *normal family* experience, with mom and dad living under the same roof. Something I hadn't had the opportunity to live myself as a kid.

But along the way, I had learned to become more in tune with my emotions and realized that it had been a long time since I had felt genuinely happy in my romantic relationship. I tried to hide it from my children and myself, until the time came when I couldn't take it anymore. Over the years, my husband and I had grown very distant. Somewhere along the way, our connection had frayed, and we had lost our way to each other. I had to release my emotions before they consumed me. I had to leave our marriage before our relationship disintegrated beyond repair.

Before having the difficult conversation, I sat quietly and began to meditate, practicing a technique I had learned about lovingly letting go. I imagined my husband wrapped in a big bubble of love energy, where he was open and receptive to my words. I was able to express my pain to him, describing the times I had felt alone raising our children and the persistent pressure I felt to be perfect. I allowed myself to express myself fully from the heart. Then, I put myself in my husband's shoes so I could understand the situation from *his* perspective. That's when I understood that he never intended to hurt me or anyone else. Like me, he tried to do the best he could with the resources he had at the time.

Afterward, I imagined holding him tenderly in my arms, lovingly forgiving him, and then gently releasing him, watching the protective bubble around him grow smaller and smaller as it drifted away. Once I emptied any feelings of anger or resentment from my being, I mustered enough courage to start the conversation I knew he and I had avoided for years.

"I want a divorce," I told him.

Although he knew this would happen at some point, the phrase took him by surprise and he asked me to reconsider my decision, wanting badly to hold on to an impossible situation for both of us and our kids.

"Let's talk about this, please give me a chance," he pleaded.

Part of me wanted to say yes. Part of me wanted to try again, but another part of me knew it was too late. Our marriage, which had once burned like a bright fire, had now been reduced to cold, wet ashes. Not a single ember remained capable of rekindling what we had once shared. I was tired of fighting. Tired of trying to live up to an unrealistic expectation of perfection. And most of all, I was tired of the mask I had to wear every day to preserve the fragile balance of our relationship. I wanted to feel alive again, to be able to wake up in peace and feel the expansion of being **ME**. The life I wanted was fundamentally different from the one I had been leading, and I felt like I could no longer breathe.

My husband finally understood. We sat down to have a heartfelt conversation, knowing that the connection through our children was unbreakable, and we were trying to make the best of a difficult situation for both of us with as much grace as possible. We made a list of how we would divide what we had, and how we would take care of our children, and we put everything on paper. We divorced a couple of months later, without involving lawyers, without third-party entanglements, and leaving the doors open to continue the cordial relationship we have to this day. At that moment, we were able to see each other as the two incredible human beings that we were and understood that it was time to fly in different directions.

After my divorce, a whole new chapter in my life began to unfold. I had been repressing parts of myself to fit into a mold that hadn't served me for years, and now I had complete freedom to live my life on my own terms. I had released the heavy weight from my wings and was ready to give them back their purpose: *to help me fly again.*

Journal Insight Questions

This is an exercise created by Vishen Lakhiani from the 6-Phase Meditation Protocol. The 6-Phase Meditation is a transcendent practice he developed to help you transform the way you think about the world, and one of the key elements of this practice is forgiveness.

This exercise is meant to *build the forgiving muscle* so you can forgive anything.

Rules of forgiveness:

- You can forgive anything and anyone.
- Forgiveness frees YOU: While it is not the same as pardoning, you decide that you are not going to let that act negatively impact you.
- Forgiveness is not about dropping the charge. You can't change the past but you can change your feelings about it.
- The other person does not have to forgive you in return.

Step 1. Pick something or someone in your life that you want to forgive.

- Think about a specific person or situation that happened in your life where you felt a negative charge. Maybe you felt hurt or resentful because of that.
  - o Choose something easy for you to forgive first, like someone cutting you in traffic in the morning; as you have more practice, you can forgive bigger things.

Step 2. Create the space for forgiveness

- Find a place where you feel safe and calm.
- Take a few deep breaths as you prepare your body and mind to be in a state of forgiveness.
- See the person that you want to forgive standing in front of you in a safe space in your mind.

Step 3. Read the charges: Tell the person how their actions made you feel.

- In your mind, tell the person exactly what they did to harm or betray you as if you were reading the charge out in court.
- Remember that you are safe now. No one can hurt you, so speak your truth freely.
- Imagine the other person is listening to you attentively.

Step 4. Allow yourself to feel the anger and pain (for no more than 2 minutes).

Step 5. See the situation from the other person's perspective.

- Now stop focusing on the pain and draw your attention to the person who wronged you again.
- Put yourself in the person's shoes for a moment and see the situation from their eyes, even if this feels difficult in the beginning.
- Remember: hurt people tend to hurt others.
- Think about how they may perceive the situation.
- You can go further and think about what they could have experienced in their life that caused them to behave this way.

Step 6. Think of what you learned in the event.

- How did the situation help you grow?
- Did this incident help you become stronger or wiser?

Step 7. Forgive into love

- Now, as you see this person in front of you, choose to forgive them. If you can, imagine hugging them as a symbol of your forgiveness.

You can repeat this process as many times as you need until you feel there is nothing else you need to forgive. You can also use this process to forgive **yourself**.

Every time you forgive, you are releasing weight from your own life. Eventually, over time, you will find that you don't need to forgive anyone anymore as you get to understand that we are all human, trying to do the best that we can with the resources we have. This makes you FREE.

CHAPTER 17

MEET YOUR INNER FAMILY

*H*ave you ever set out to do something out of your comfort zone, start very excited about the idea of doing something new, and right when you are about to do it, the *"little voices in your head"* make you question yourself?

For example:

- You finally decide to put yourself out there and post that video on social media about that message close to your heart. But as you are uploading it, you start to doubt your worth, and you end up not sharing your message.
- You prepare for a difficult conversation that you have been putting off for the longest time, and right before you are going to have it, you start to think about all the things that can go wrong, so you keep quiet.
- You book time for yourself to get a massage because you want to get pampered, but on the way to the spa, you start to feel guilty about taking time away from others, and you end up cancelling your appointment.

Sounds familiar? Well, you are not alone!

We are complex beings you and I, and like all humans, we entertain around 60,000 thoughts in a day. The good thing is that these thoughts are just parts of our *inner system* to keep us *safe*. These are just different parts of our being that give us an opinion on what is the best course for us to take. So start by recognizing that the parts of your personality are just that—a *part* of who you are that lives in your mind as a thought. The parts don't define your *whole*; they simply reflect something you need to pay attention to at the moment.

I call these parts the "Inner Family".

This is the story about how I got reintroduced to my inner family: I was slowly getting used to being a single mom while raising my two teenage kids, trying to do the best I could. Avi, my youngest daughter, was navigating the challenging landscape of adolescence, and it seemed like we often butted heads. I was trying to be a *good mom* and set healthy boundaries, while she was trying to figure out how to go from being a child to becoming an adult. All of this occurred while she was dealing with her own grief over her parents' separation and the fact that she couldn't see her dad as often as she wanted.

I had urged my ex-husband to align our parenting efforts for the sake of our children, especially since I had them in my care 95% of the time, but he constantly found ways to contradict me to please the kids. One day, a major argument broke out between my daughter and me over a party she wanted to go to. After I firmly said no, she called her dad to try to change his decision. He, of course, said yes, like he always did.

"This is my house and you are going to follow my rules as long as you live under my roof," I stated.

"Well, if that's the way it is, then I'm going to go live with my dad," my daughter responded.

I felt like my heart was squeezed into a small ball. I felt deeply hurt and resentful. After all, *I had been the one who had taken care of her throughout her life. I was the one who nurtured her, took her to school, cooked for her every day, took her to dance classes, and supported her every step she took. And yet she wanted to go live with her dad. OUCH!*

But I had grown tired of getting caught in the crossfire of the *good cop-bad cop* dynamic. I was tired of being the one who constantly set limits, and conversely, her dad was often seen as the permissive and understanding one.

I thought, *"Of course, it's easier for him! He only sees the kids every couple of months, while I'm responsible for their daily education."* So I grabbed a suitcase and asked my daughter to pack her things. Then we got in the car and took her to my ex's apartment. His jaw nearly hit the floor in shock when he saw us with suitcases. He had never anticipated becoming a responsible full-time father of a teenage girl. He never expected me to get tired of the game and take action.

When I dropped my daughter off at her dad's house, my heart sank. I cried the entire 30-minute ride back home, feeling defeated and empty. After spending the next 5 days drowning my sorrows in wine and tears, I knew I had to act. So since I'm quite impulsive, I signed up for a 10-day Vipassana retreat without reading what that implied. It was a retreat of absolute silence designed to help you go within and heal. This was exactly what I needed at that moment (or so I thought).

I packed my things and drove three hours to the place where I would spend the next 10 days immersed in nature and silence. I arrived at the retreat center feeling triumphant. I had been preparing for this experience for years. Working at a personal development company, I felt completely up to the challenge. I happily handed over all my possessions to the person at the front desk. She then explained that I could not talk, make eye contact with others, read, write, or do any activity that could create a distraction to *clear my mind*. I accepted the conditions and then went to my room to prepare for my inner journey.

The next day, they woke us up at 4 in the morning. It was dark, but the sky was incredibly beautiful. Being far from the city, and in the absence of busy spaces, I was able to see the immensity of the sky adorned with thousands and thousands of stars. It reminded me of the sense of wonder I had felt in Cambodia. We then entered the meditation room to observe our breathing in silence. Two hours passed and I felt like a champ! We were then taken to the breakfast area to eat oatmeal and fruit. Life was good for me! Before moving on to the next meditation session, I went to my room to take a bath. The water was freezing, and I wanted to scream because it felt like my body was under attack. But I managed to keep my composure in silence. I still felt strong.

The next two-hour meditation session was not so easy. The guide told us to focus on our breathing again. My mind started to tantrum: *AGAIN? But we did this just a few hours ago!* I tried to sit still in silence, but I was bored and my back hurt. The second session seemed like an eternity, and we had two more sessions of silence left before the day was over.

Everything started going downhill from there.

I knew I had an overactive mind, but not being able to talk about it made my thoughts incredibly loud. I found myself thinking about everything at the same time and at full volume. As the days went by, things got worse. I felt very angry when the guide told us to focus on our breathing once again. I was able to experience ALL the feelings except the promised *peace* I was supposed to feel.

I tried to make eye contact with the other people at the retreat, but it was forbidden, so I looked for other ways to stay calm, from watching ants eat an entire plant and take the pieces back to their nest, to rearranging all of the stones near the river bank in symmetrical patterns.

On the fourth day, I had already lost my sanity. I went into *survival mode* and began exploring the riverbank for possible ways to escape my *prison of peace*. I even considered leaving my car stranded. I just needed to escape from that place! I got to the river and saw a huge stone. Something inside me called me toward going to the stone, so I followed my intuition. (I had nothing else to do anyway.) I hugged the stone and started crying: *WHAT THE HELL AM I DOING HERE?!* I screamed.

In my head, the stone answered that I was there because I needed to find my peace. Even though I felt like a crazy person for having a conversation with a stone, I had one of the deepest conversations of my life with it, and allowed myself to cry as much as I needed to cry.

When I had nothing more to release, I sat on the stone and made myself comfortable. I realized that it was time to make friends with the many voices inside my head. The different sides of my personality that make up who I am. I had suppressed these voices for so long that when I finally gave them the chance to speak, they all demanded attention at once, wanting to share what they had been withholding my entire life.

It was an unbearable feeling, especially because I couldn't do anything other than be still and quiet. I pleaded for their silence, promising them that I would give them all the attention they required with the condition that only one of them could speak at a time. This is when I finally allowed all the members of my *inner family* to come and have a heartfelt conversation with me. The first one I had allowed them to have in years, and the first of many more to come.

My inner perfectionist was the first to arrive. She was worried about this new *"woo-woo"* side of me. She felt afraid that I would stop planning every detail because we could get lost. She presented me with a flow chart to clearly explain all the things that could go wrong with this *go-with-the-flow* madness and how our productivity could go down the drain. I gave her a glass of organic wine, smiled at her, and asked her to relax for once in her life, assuring her that everything would be fine. She opened her mouth to respond, but for the first time, she was left speechless. She went to the corner of my mind and took a sip of wine.

My inner saboteur was sitting in front of me completely furious. She crossed her arms and asked me in a critical tone: *"Who do you think you are to want a life like that? You are not a guru; you are not a millionaire, and you also have a ton of responsibilities. How do you think you are going to achieve all these things that you now say you want?"* I laughed out loud when I saw her frowning face, and I simply said, "It's ME and that's enough!" I gave her a glass of wine as well and sent her to sit with my inner perfectionist so they could discuss as much as they wanted, out of my sight.

Once they were both gone, the lighter parts of me felt more welcome to show up. My inner child chimed in. She was now a happy, confident, loud child who knew her voice mattered. She came to remind me that life is too precious not to enjoy every little moment of the day. She asked me to live more in the present and stop worrying so much about what would come next. She also reminded me to play.

My inner creativity brought me colors and the collection of carefully bound dreams that I had long put aside. She was excited to start working again on projects that were aligned with my heart, mapping out a series of ideas she had in mind for us to do.

My inner warrior came to remind me of my strength. To show me all the obstacles and trials I had overcome in my life, and to celebrate the fact that I always kept moving forward. She celebrated my perseverance for never giving up, and she told me that she was ready to be by my side, to overcome any challenges that came our way.

And finally, my inner wisdom arrived. She had been sitting silently, observing all the conversations with the different parts of me. She took my hands and simply said: *"One day at a time, France. You got this!"*

I survived the rest of my silent retreat with a little more peace; I stopped running away from my thoughts and learned to listen to the different parts of me without judging.

A month after I returned home from the Vipassana retreat, my daughter moved back home, and our relationship completely changed. We learned to communicate with more love and grace between the two of us.

I'm far from perfect and I have no intention of trying. But I have healed that in me. I have learned to give myself the same grace, love, and understanding that I offer everyone else in my life. I am in the process of learning to choose my battles more wisely, focus my energy on what I want to expand, release what no longer serves me with lightness in my heart, and take one step forward at a time. I do this knowing in my heart that I am doing the best I can with the resources available to me.

And that, my friend, is **good enough**. So allow yourself to release any burden that you carry by accepting all the parts that make you who you are as each one of those parts is a unique feather of yours, each of them necessary to build your unique wings.

Journal Insight Questions

Take a moment to meet the members of your *inner family,* and give each part of who you are a chance to say what they need to say to you.

Think of something new that you want to try. Something out of your comfort zone or something just for *you*. Notice what comes up for you when you think about doing this thing.

- What are the thoughts that come to mind?
- What are the different parts of yourself trying to tell you?
- What are they trying to protect you from?

When you finish giving your inner family members their chance to speak, thank them for their message, understand where they are coming from, and release them into love.

CHAPTER **18**

WELCOME
ALL YOUR
EMOTIONS

*W*e have a natural tendency to shy away from things that make us uncomfortable because our entire system is designed to protect us. Once we go through a situation that makes us feel pain or insecurity, the brain stores that information in our cells, so the next time we receive a *danger signal,* our body alerts us to flee. This is great for protecting you from *real* danger.

The problem arises when your natural alerts are masked by beliefs you have about a situation that *may* happen based on your perception of past experiences. What you think affects how you feel, and this in turn affects how you show up in the world and what you do.

We tend to avoid feeling uncomfortable. Avoid any emotion that we have labeled as *bad* by turning off our *emotional switch* so we don't experience discomfort. Disassociating ourselves from situations that feel out of our control, or finding alternate ways to distract us from confronting the emotions that we don't want to feel. But if you *turn off your emotional switch* to avoid the uncomfortable, you will also turn off the switch to feel anything else, including joy and happiness.

Running away from uncomfortable emotions only makes them louder because emotions are just *energy in motion* that needs to move and give you a message. Once you're able to stop and face your emotions, you'll discover that many times, that thing you've been running away from isn't so scary after all.

I spent a couple of years enjoying my alone time after my divorce. It was a time of self-discovery and personal growth, a journey to learn to be single, to know, accept, and love myself completely. I needed to heal old patterns, develop areas of my life I had never explored before, and most importantly, I learned to feel comfortable in my own skin.

A part of me was reluctant to *expose myself* again, for fear of suffering. However, another part of me craved a connection. Finally, I got to a point where I felt ready to leave the comfort of my home and *put myself out there* again. But as I did, I found a completely new and different world than the one I had known when I was 20 (before I got married for the first time). I, too, had changed a lot since then, and I realized that I no longer liked bars, noisy places, or crowded spaces.

So I decided to start slow on the romantic side and focus on building friendships. I started going to friends' houses for get-togethers and slowly became more comfortable in social settings. I felt at ease among friends, but when someone tried to romantically approach me, I felt an invisible wall rising from within, and my legs preparing to flee the scene. I also recognized that my tendency to run away from intimacy was not going to serve me well in the satisfying long-term relationships I wanted.

My friends called me one day to tell me about a shaman who led Ayahuasca ceremonies in the Talamanca mountains in Limón. I found Ayahuasca intriguing but intimidating as I saw it as a gateway to the unknown. They insisted that I try it and invited me to open up to the experience. As the curious researcher that I am, I studied more about this medicinal plant and its potential to reveal aspects of oneself that conventional therapies often couldn't reach.

After years of personal growth work, I felt it was time to confront my "*chronic escapism*" based on my fear of getting hurt. I took the leap and joined a group of four close friends to live the experience. We embarked on a month-long preparation to align our bodies and minds to receive the medicine.

When the day of the ceremony arrived, we drove for 4 hours and then walked another 2 through the mountains to reach the shaman's remote location. The mountain was incredible. It was huge, clean, and full of the most wonderful energy. The shaman had cultivated his Ayahuasca plants for decades, planting them with his own hands.

At the top of the mountain, we reached the place where the ceremony would take place. The shaman had prepared some mattresses for us to spend the night outdoors, surrounded by the immensity of the sky. He prepared a unique mix of plants adapted to each of our intentions. He asked us to trust the process and open ourselves to receive and embrace everything that the plant wanted to reveal to us.

Before beginning the ceremony, the shaman gave us a space to discuss our intentions for the Ayahuasca experience. I had no idea what my intention was at that moment. The only thing I knew was that the plant had somehow *called me* to heal a part of me that was hidden. I needed to see it so I could release it. This simple sense of the need to discover was enough for the shaman, and it was all I had to offer. I saw my friends receive the medicine and retreat to their designated places to start the experience, while I awaited my turn for what felt like forever.

Then finally, I was called. The shaman gave me my dose of Ayahuasca, I grabbed the tiny cup in my hands and took a sip. The taste was bitter and sour, but I swallowed it anyway. We had fasted all day, expecting a physical and mental purge. However, I was not hungry; my being was solely focused on the profound message that I was about to receive and that would change my life.

I began to feel anxious, urging my body to open and receive because I was READY! But the only thing I could feel was that my eyelids were getting heavier and heavier. Then my arms, and then my whole body. It was like someone had poured cement on me.

It took all my energy to get up and walk towards the Shaman.

"I need help," I said.

"What happened?" he asked.

"I am ready to receive my message and see the visions that are meant for me to see, but I feel so tired. I want to sleep."

"Then sleep," he said.

"But I…"

His smile left no room for argument and my body needed sleep. I went to my mattress and told myself I would take a short nap so I could be prepared for the messages and life-changing visions I had heard so many others experience before.

When I woke up from *"my nap"*, it was already 6:00 am the next day. I looked around and found everyone from the ceremony sleeping soundly. I panicked for a moment because that meant I had missed the whole experience!

My heart raced, and I felt like a loser. All that preparation for nothing. I had literally slept all night! I approached my friends and urged them to wake up so we could leave. I needed to get away from that place. They had been up all night, and they asked me to relax before they went back to sleep. Every cell in my body was screaming for me to leave the mountain. I felt extremely uncomfortable in my own skin. However, no one responded to my pleas, so I went for a walk to leave my discomfort in nature.

As I walked through the forest, I felt a lump in my throat that grew larger and larger, like a living entity seeking to escape my body. I ran as far away from the camp as possible and hid within the trees, where I finally let my tears flow freely. I couldn't understand why I was crying, but I needed to release something in me.

And *then* I understood it.

The goal of the experience was to confront my constant desire to escape the feeling of discomfort. The last parts of me that needed to have everything under control to feel safe, and the constant comparison I subjected myself to, which always made me feel like something was *missing*. I cried in the arms of the trees that fed my soul and allowed me to unload without judging. I learned to be comfortable being uncomfortable, knowing that there was nowhere I could run away from my own emotions and that it was okay for me to just BE.

The incredible freedom it gives you to welcome all your emotions and all the parts of you that show up is enormous. When you learn to love everything that makes up the beautiful human that you ARE, then life becomes easier. You will find less resistance to trying new things, become more confident, and release the heavy weight of your overthinking mind that tries to label every experience, so that you can focus on actually *living*.

Feel the wings on your back getting lighter already!

Journal Insight Questions & Action Steps

This tool will help you get comfortable with ALL your emotions. Any one of them that decides to show up and give you a message. All I ask of you before you try it is to remove your *label maker* from this exercise (no judging). Remove the need to catalog your experience as good or bad based on preconceptions that you have, and be open to welcoming all your emotions.

This technique is called RAIN, and it's a practice developed by Tara Brach, a psychologist and meditation teacher. It is a 4-step process that will help you manage the emotions that you tend to run away from. So the next time you are experiencing something that feels uncomfortable, you feel the need to flee, disassociate, or distract yourself with something to avoid feeling your emotion. STOP. Take a breath and try this:

Step 1. Recognize: Recognize and acknowledge the presence of the emotion you're experiencing without judgment or resistance. Simply notice the emotion as it arises—whether it's sadness, anger, fear, or any other feeling.

Imagine your emotion knocking at the door of your consciousness. Asking to be let in because it has a message for you.

Step 2. Allow: Once you've recognized the emotion, allow yourself to fully experience it without trying to suppress or avoid it. This step involves permitting yourself to feel whatever you're feeling, even if it's uncomfortable or painful. Instead of pushing the emotion away, create space for it to be present in your awareness.

This is when you invite your emotion into your *"inner living room"* so you can be together in a more intimate space and your emotion can communicate what it needs to tell you.

Step 3. Investigate: With a sense of curiosity and openness, investigate the emotion more closely. Pay attention to where you feel it in your body, the thoughts and beliefs associated with it, and any other sensations or images that arise. This step involves exploring the emotion with gentle curiosity, allowing you to deepen your understanding of it.

Here are some questions that will help you investigate your emotions deeper:

- Where do you feel the emotion in your body?
- What size or texture do you feel around this emotion?
- If your emotion had a color, what color would it be?
- Do you sense a temperature?
- What is your emotion trying to tell you?
- What does it need to be released?

Step 4. Nurture: Finally, nurture yourself with kindness and compassion. Offer yourself the same care and support you would offer to a friend who's struggling. This step involves responding to yourself with warmth and understanding, soothing the discomfort of the emotion, and offering yourself the comfort and reassurance you need.

You can imagine yourself hugging your emotion, thanking it for the lesson or message it brought to you, and then gently allowing it to dissolve back where it came from. Sense it getting smaller and smaller as it drifts away.

PART 5

Be Present

The only real place from where we can create our reality is when we are fully in the PRESENT moment.

We cannot create anything from our past because it no longer exists, and all we can do is learn from it.

Nor can we create anything from our future. It hasn't happened yet, and all it does is fill our experience with anxiety about what we don't know is going to happen.

Being fully in the present heals our past by recognizing that it is no longer there, and allows us to build our future from a place of possibility rather than uncertainty.

The present is the place where we connect to our wings. Where we remember that we have the power to choose our destiny based on the choices that we make in every moment.

"The moment is not found by seeking it,
but by ceasing to escape from it."

– James Pierce

CHAPTER 19

CONNECT TO
THE NOW

*L*earning to be okay with being present is a huge turning point, especially in a fast-moving world characterized by constant competition and endless distractions. We have too many things fighting for our attention at all moments, and we are always glued to a device that keeps us *up to date* with the latest news. There are so many things to do that require us to be *in action* all the time, and so many goals we feel we have to achieve to live *our ideal life,* that being present feels like *a waste of our precious time* as we fall into the comparison game with what everyone else is doing. Always feeling behind *someone* or *something.*

This is something curious about our human nature and the way we think. We tend to contradict what we SAY we want with what we actually DO. We all long to connect to others on some level, but when we have real people in front of us, we dive into distractions to keep us *busy.*

Our body is constantly in one place, and our mind in another, so we continuously feel like we are divided. We work our whole lives so that when we reach the end of our days, we can truly enjoy our time with our loved ones, and yet we never cultivate our relationships or our health, so when we finally retire, there are fewer positive experiences to be had.

Every day creates your future based on your choices. So instead of racing toward the next goal or finding ways to escape the *real world,* choose to be present in whatever life brings you in the moment. Being present allows you to focus your energy and attention on one thing at a time, reducing anxiety and overwhelm, and allowing you to feel more calm when you approach anything in your life.

Being present allows you to connect to your wings. Fully feel them in your being. It also allows you to notice the feathers that are all around, behind every experience that you have. These feathers can only be collected when you pause long enough to see them.

When you constantly push yourself to DO more without giving yourself permission to just BE, you eventually fall into **burnout**. And this is not because you are weak, but rather because this is the way that your biology is designed. You NEED breaks. Moments of not doing anything. These are the moments when your brain and your body repair and heal. And these breaks shouldn't only happen when you sleep, but it's also important to have these moments of pause during your day so you can be present.

I know about burnout all too well because I've always been extremely competitive. My whole life had been like an *all-in* poker game, and I had no idea how to do anything half-heartedly, so when I couldn't get maximum results (and fast), I became very frustrated.

Thinking about my soul before being born, I pictured myself as the *nerd soul* in Heaven who always had her hand raised to volunteer for everything so that when she was reincarnated on Earth, she would be fully prepared. I imagined my soul negotiating with the guides to achieve a *many-lives-in-one* deal to accelerate my karmic journey on Earth. I found this very funny, but the irony is that constant running had been a part of my personality for as long as I can remember. Once I achieved one goal, I would immediately set my sights on the next, never allowing myself a moment to savor the present.

One Sunday afternoon in August, I poured myself a cup of hot coffee and sat on the terrace watching the heavy rain pouring down on the garden. I was thinking about my future and the next goals I was going to set for the month. With my legs stretched out on the chair, I noticed my sneakers and suddenly remembered a Nike ad from the 80s.

The ad showed a female athlete preparing for a marathon. Determined and focused, she put on her running shoes and spent the rest of the ad running in different settings, sprinting incessantly without ever taking a break. The ad asked a question at the end: *"What are you training for?"*

I put aside all other thoughts and paid attention to that question: *What was I training for? I was constantly running, but to create what? What was that end goal that I wanted to create that required me to always be doing something?* I knew I wanted to create a positive impact on the world. My big purpose was to help 100,000 people on their journey of self-discovery and transformation. That seemed like too big and important a task to take *easily*. But *was it really good for me to be always busy non-stop?*

On the other hand, I also wanted to create an extraordinary life where I could enjoy myself and build beautiful relationships along my path. And for that to happen, I needed to allow myself to stop my *to-do* train and be present. I then realized that a big part of what I wanted was to savor life instead of running after it.

I grew up in a big Latin American family, on a family property with my grandparents' home in the middle, and all my aunts and uncles built around it. It was a beautiful experience to grow up with my tribe, with access to unlimited play dates with my cousins out in the big garden, savoring the afternoons sitting in a mango tree, running after the squirrels that lived in the forest, or discovering the treasures that lay below the bird nests.

Our grandparents Luisa and Rodrigo were the center of our family life. Their home was the usual hanging out place where we all came for unlimited hugs, food, and comfort. We spent so many moments in that home, shared so many stories, and witnessed generations after generations of new family members come into the world and grow together.

But as we grew older and started accumulating life responsibilities, we drifted apart. Each one of us was dedicated to our careers and families. Each of us getting busier as our lives grew more complex. We kept seeing each other on special Holidays, and some afternoon coffee sessions, but long gone were the deep connection adventures from our childhood.

Then my grandfather passed away, and my grandmother had to learn to live her life on her own after raising a family of six children, nineteen grandchildren, and many great-grandchildren. We visited her as often as we could. Fighting against our busy schedules, making room for her along with the life goals we each pursued. Each visit to her home was delicious because she was always so present. She was such a beautiful witness to our story, always listening from the heart, making us feel like we were the most important person in the world when we were with her. She gave us permission to pause the to-dos and just BE perfectly imperfect without judgment.

One December afternoon, my grandma Luisa called my entire family to her home. She asked us all to leave anything else aside for that time as she needed to talk to all of us. We gathered in her living room, a large group of humans bound by blood and shared history. My grandma allowed time for us to catch up with each other first. Then she informed us that she had been diagnosed with terminal liver cancer. The news hit us hard. My grandmother had been the rock for all of us, and we didn't know how to live life without her.

She told us that she was very happy with the way she had lived her life and had no regrets. Then she asked us all to celebrate the time she had left in her physical body to the fullest without any medical treatments that would steal her final moments of joy. During her last month, we put aside our hectic lives and obligations to immerse ourselves in quality time with her. We walked through the rich tapestry of stories from our lives, shared meals, hugged each other, engaged in soul-stirring conversations, and laughed a lot.

As a family, we bonded in a way that altered each of us forever. We rediscovered the art of being fully present, free of any expectations other than the simple fact of being there.

When her time came, my grandmother died peacefully in her sleep, surrounded by her loved ones. She felt no pain, she knew no fear, and she left us all the priceless gift of her presence and a deep gratitude for her existence in our lives.

It was such a sad but beautiful way to make friends with grief. To learn to put things in perspective so we can focus on what really matters, to stop running to the *next thing* without savoring where you are, and to know that the only moment that matters is right NOW.

So while you are here on Earth, listen to your heart, allow your emotions to surface when necessary, and let your thoughts flow. Instead of judging yourself, become an observer of your life and consciously choose how you want to respond. Life is a precious thing, so decide to take every moment as a gift. Every experience is a feather that will help you build your magnificent wings!

Journal Insight Questions and Action Steps

I am going to share with you one of the most powerful practices to help you be fully present. And no, it is not meditation (although it works wonders!) This is a practice of gratitude.

Gratitude brings your focus to what you appreciate in your experience right now. Not on what you lack, or want to create in the future, but what you have now. It brings your attention to the present moment and helps you feel more calm, happy, and connected with yourself and others.

Every day, before you start your day, take 5 minutes to practice gratitude:

- Think about 3 things you are grateful for in your life. What you appreciate from your everyday experience.
- Think about 3 things that you are grateful for about yourself as a person. Things you like about your character and personality.
- Then, think about 3 things that you are grateful for in your career, your vocation, or your purpose

This is a happiness booster that will completely shift your day!

Children see magic because they look for it."

– Christopher Moore

Chapter 20

THE WISE
TEACHINGS
OF THE
MINI-MENTORS

*A*s we grow up, we tend to complicate the way we understand life. We immerse ourselves in books, courses, seminars, and retreats, we learn to label everything that comes our way and to put meaning in every little situation that happens. But when we reach the maturity stage of our lives, we look back and understand that the true value of our path lies in simplicity. This simplicity is available to all of us. We know in our hearts how to see things simply; we just forget it over the years as we place layers on top of layers of complicated meaning that blind us from the truth.

One of the most remarkable toys that my kids had when they were young was a cardboard box. We were celebrating Christmas with my family at my grandmother's home. We all had spent so much money buying cool toys for the kids and spent so much time wrapping them beautifully under the tree, and yet there was one thing that made their night (and the following weeks).

My grandmother had to buy a new washing machine for her home. It had come just a couple of days before Christmas, but the box was still in her garage waiting for the recycling truck to take it away. While we were preparing dinner for the family, the children went to my grandmother's garage to play and found the giant cardboard box. They brought pillows and blankets to turn the box into a fort and spent the rest of the night happily playing inside.

I have met many incredible teachers and mentors in my years of being on this planet. They all taught me incredible lessons about life, helped me create new knowledge, and take the next steps in my journey. But I wanted to find a way to be more present in the moment and be able to notice all the little things. This was key to finding my feathers and connecting to my wings. I was looking to understand how to make the everyday moments of my life more noticeable, and then I realized that the wisest mentors were available to help me do it.

The most profound lessons I have received in my life did not come from experts or specialists; instead, they have been gifted with the humble wisdom of children. So I made a conscious effort to immerse myself in their world, intentionally spending time in their presence, observing and learning from them. Children love simplicity. It is we, as adults, who begin to complicate life!

Children have a special way of teaching. They don't give you a lecture on how you should live your life, but rather they show you. So I purposefully set aside time to be in their presence and just watch them hang out and play.

Below are some of the things I learned from them:

1.   *Get out of Your Head*

Children don't waste their valuable time overthinking anything. They haven't had enough layers of *labels* installed in their consciousness to put meaning into each situation as we adults do. They don't have plans, goals, vision boards, or to-do lists. They live in the moment to the fullest. They simply show up and respond to what shows up in the moment. So stop trying to be an expert and enjoy what comes. Send your *Inner label maker* to the trash!

2.   *Listen to Your Body*

Children are truly connected to their bodies and totally in tune with their needs. They don't eat because they have to. They eat when they are hungry and look for the food their body needs at that moment. They permit themselves to live their emotions, and they seek constant movement to stay healthy and give their bodies rest when they need to recharge.

Connect to your body and attune to what it needs. This will help you feel energized and nourished so you can then create your days from a full tank of possibilities.

3.   *LOVE Unconditionally*

Children don't care about the color of your skin, your religion, your age, or your titles. They will love you fully for who you are without any judgment and without holding back. They understand that we are all created from the same source, and they will love you for the mere fact that you exist.

When was the last time that you loved another person unconditionally? How about loving yourself that way? Take your ego out of the equation and remember that we are all ONE. We all come from the same place, but we are all living different life experiences so that we can see the world from all possible perspectives!

4.   *Look for Awe in Everything*

Everything is new to the eyes of a small child. Everything they see is a discovery, and they explore the world from a place of curiosity, like endless adventurers who discover new treasures with every step they take. Children actively seek wonder. They are open to the experience of seeing everything around them as a new opportunity for enjoyment. This not only helps them be extremely grateful, but it also helps them be grounded.

Actively look for your feathers in everything that you do. The feathers represent the moments of magic that are always available to you in your days. The beautiful sunrise, the sound of birds that remind you that everything is alive, the colors of the flowers that brighten up your life… Everything out there is a miracle, and when you purposefully look for awe in everything, your brain will scan your environment to find it.

5. *Get Curious and Question Everything*

Why? Why? Why? This repetitive question that can sometimes bother us as adults is how children make sense of the world around them. They don't take things for granted just because you say so. They question everything to truly understand how the world works.

As adults, we are indoctrinated into accepting everything society tells us, what the guru of the moment says, and what experts claim to be true, but we rarely ask ourselves if these *truths* are real. Question everything, and this will help you remove the limiting labels that stop you from being free. It will also allow your uniqueness to surface!

6. *Have Fun and Do What Makes Your Heart Sing*

Fun is a high vibrational frequency that elevates your state. It also triggers the release of endorphins, the body's natural chemicals that make us feel good. Children make sure to invest as much as they can each day into things that make them feel good, while we, as adults, somehow seek the opposite. We are glued to the news, feeding on messages that only serve to create fear and despair.

Purposefully change your focus and everything else will change with it. Remember that your energy flows where your attention goes, so focus your energy on what moves you and what makes you want to sing, dance, or celebrate. Do something you love every single day, and watch how your wings start to vibrate stronger.

7. *Always Stick to the Truth*

When we are programmed to be people pleasers, we somehow feel that telling the truth is equivalent to hurting someone. And this is not true! Children are honest and always say what they think according to how they perceive the truth. As adults, we tend to create entire stories of our version of reality. We make up stories about people we don't know and believe that our perception is the *"only"* reality that exists.

Instead, become curious and learn to see how other people perceive their world, rather than constructing complicated stories of how you think it is. Connect to what you really want to say, and allow your heart to speak its truth, while also respecting other people's ways of communicating their own version of it.

8. *Allow Your Emotions to Flow*

Children's emotions need to flow, and they allow themselves to feel what they need to feel before letting it go and moving on with their day. They do not avoid feeling or hide their emotions under *the mental rug;* they simply allow themselves to be. Once their emotion is fully expressed, they continue with their day without the heaviness of internal judgment.

As adults, we tend to suppress our emotions to avoid feeling uncomfortable, or to avoid making others feel uncomfortable. But this doesn't allow us to be fully free. So embrace your emotions, dance with them, allow them to flow through you, and then move on. Free yourself from the shackles of trying to fit into a model of how you are supposed to be, and just allow yourself to be human.

9. *Forgive with Ease*

Children know how to let things go with love. They get into a fight with someone, and 5 minutes later, they're friends again. They forgive easily and do not hold grudges because they know life is too precious to waste energy on fights that contribute nothing.

Choose your fights wisely, and remember that not everything that happens that you don't agree with is a war. Let go of the heaviness of holding grudges because, in the end, the only person that gets hurt by that is you!

Action Steps

This is a very simple but profound exercise that will teach you more about life than what you can learn in many of the books, seminars, or growth programs that you will find out there. The exercise is to witness a child for a couple of hours.

You can spend time with family or friends who have small children, or even spend time looking at your own kids if they are young. Leave your to-dos at home, put your phone away for those two hours, and just observe the child. Notice how they are fully immersed in the moment, see how curious they get about the most simple thing in life, and savor their laughter as they play.

Then play along with them! Immerse yourself into their world of unlimited creativity, paint pictures of unicorns in the sky, and allow them to guide you into a unique experience of seeing the world through their eyes. Walk with them through a path that is still free from labels and limitations, and then feel how your own wings start to move.

CHAPTER 21

ACTIVELY PURSUE JOY

*W*e know exactly when we were born, but we have no idea when we are going to die. So if life is such a precious gift, why not spend more time enjoying all of its little moments?

We tend to focus on the big goals we have in life. In the many things we want to achieve for the future, when the true gift of life is in the small moments that connect the dots of where we are today and where we envision ourselves to be.

Remember, actively pursuing joy doesn't mean ignoring negative emotions or pretending that everything is *perfect*. It's about consciously choosing activities and experiences that bring you happiness and fulfillment, even in the middle of life's challenges.

Everything is made up of energy, from the trees to the birds, to your body, and even your thoughts. Joy is a high-vibrational energy. This means that when you consciously do something that you really enjoy doing, you are attuning all your energy to that high-vibrational energy. Not only do you reap the benefits by feeling amazing, having better health, and a clearer mind, but also the people around you will feel this and benefit too!

Every time you connect to your joy, you will show up differently for yourself and others. You will be less judgmental, more relaxed, and more open to receiving the gifts that life has for you. Book time in your calendar to do something that you love every day, to try a new hobby, or to explore something new. Let go of the things that don't make you feel expansive, and forgive yourself with grace.

I begin my days with a simple mantra: my personal contract that outlines my daily commitments so that my focus is always on the things that serve ME the best. It's something like this:

"For the next 24 hours, I promise to myself:

- To feed my mind with the thoughts that serve me and let go of the thoughts that don't.
- To nourish my body with the best nutrients and choose foods that serve me.
- To give my body movement so it stays healthy and strong.
- To create space to share with the people who I love and who matter to me.
- To show up in my work with the energy of love and service in every task I do.
- To open my heart to give and receive abundantly.
- To find a space to do something today that makes my heart sing."

This contract helps me focus my energy on a deeper question: *What if this was my last day on Earth? What would I love to do today?*

One thing I have learned about myself, especially after my Vipassana experience, is that I don't enjoy being still. While I admire those who can sit quietly, clear their minds, and simply breathe, that approach is not for me. I wanted a practice that would help me be present in the moment and, at the same time, allow me to move my body. That's how I found gardening. Throughout my life, everything I did always seemed to have an end goal. Each step was meant to achieve something more. But gardening was completely different; it was something I wanted to explore guided solely by the passion of doing it.

My lifelong fascination with plants finally had a place to flourish during the pandemic. I had always loved butterflies and dreamed of having my morning coffee surrounded by these beautiful creatures that symbolize transformation. For the first six months of 2020, I immersed myself fully in the world of gardening, experimenting with different strategies, and losing a few plants along the way, until I discovered the right amount of water, sunlight, and nutrients they needed to grow.

Six months of digging, exploring local plant nurseries, testing different flower species, and a lot of learning went into building the flower dome where my butterflies could come and have breakfast with me. This daily ritual of sipping my coffee while watching the butterflies became my morning meditation. Gardening, pruning, and caring for plants became my afternoon release routine.

Eager to experience more of this deep sense of joy, I extended my gardening passion to growing food. I built a greenhouse and started growing organic vegetables for myself and my family. Over the next two years, I built and refined many versions of my greenhouse to ensure I produced a bountiful harvest. I learned to use a machete, got a yellow wheelbarrow, and learned to fight pests using garlic and cinnamon.

I developed a deep connection with my plants by being present every day, understanding where they liked to grow best, how many times to water them, how to grow seedlings, and what they needed to grow into healthy adult plants.

What I initially saw as a hobby soon revealed its profound impact on other areas of my life. The time I spent in my garden didn't just help me grow food or attract butterflies. It taught me patience and resilience; it helped me be more present in the moment and explore new horizons based on my passions.

I finally understood the phrase, *"You bring all aspects of your life into your coaching."* I use so many gardening metaphors with my clients now. When they get frustrated because they want a result to come faster, I remind them of the time it takes a seedling to grow into a plant. Or when they feel overwhelmed with work or life's chores, I remind them that pruning out the branches of a tree that no longer serves is a great way to liberate energy so that the tree can grow stronger.

Journal Insight Questions and Action Steps

Time to play, my friend! This exercise is meant to reconnect you with your joy. :)

Go to a place where you feel comfortable, and take your journal with you.

Part 1. Understand What Brings You Joy

- Start by visualizing what joy means for you.
- How does it feel in your body?
- What thoughts come to you when you are filled with joy?
- Write down the things you loved to do as a kid.
- What are the things that you really enjoy doing?
- What are some of the activities that you want to try but have never given yourself time to try them?
- If you had unlimited resources, what would you love to experience?

Part 2. Schedule Joy Into Your Calendar

Now that you have more clarity on what joy means for you, take out your calendar, and book time every day to do something that you love, just for the sheer pleasure of doing it.

You can also bring joy into some of the activities that you already have, and just change the intention. For example, you can turn cooking from a chore that you *have to do* to a discovery session of some new flavors that you want to try or turn your daily morning shower into a dance session.

CHAPTER 22

FALL IN LOVE WITH YOUR BODY

*O*ur body is the vessel that holds our energy. We can have the best vision for our lives and the most incredible purpose, but without a body that matches the magnitude of what we want to create, there is not much we can achieve. Our health determines what we do every day and fuels our dreams, and it's just as important to work on your mind to positively affect your body as it is to work on your body to positively affect your mind. Everything is *interconnected*, and you cannot expand one area of your life without expanding the other.

I see so many people struggling with their bodies for such a big part of their lives, myself included! So many of my clients, friends, and family members trying to force their body into something it's not. Some want to lose weight and are always looking to start the *"new diet"*. Others struggle to gain weight because they feel weak. But the common theme is that most people are unhappy with their bodies.

There are several studies out there that talk about this fact. Some say that up to 90% of women worldwide have had a negative image of their body, in many cases starting at the young age of 10. This is especially alarming in the era dominated by Social Media and the unrealistic beauty standards that the influencers are setting. Just open Instagram, and there you will find thousands of *perfect* women, portraying *perfect* bodies. What you don't see is the amount of filters and special effects that their photos have to go through before they are posted. And this body image battle has been going on for years, making us feel *not good enough* when we don't fit the external standards of beauty.

I remember that during my elementary years, I was always bullied at school because I was *"the fat girl"*. My weight somehow gave permission to others to freely shame me, and my classmates called me hurtful names like *"Miss Piggy"* and *"Shamu."* The teachers didn't do anything to protect me, because it was *my fault* I was fat. Food was both my enemy and my temptation. It was a form of self-punishment that kept me tied to a body I never fully accepted.

I vividly remember my sixth-grade graduation, where I put on all the belts I had around my waist to try to hide my belly. I spent the entire graduation ceremony uncomfortable, trying to find a way to breathe, feeling the deep pain of trying to fit my body into a mold that was not mine.

As I grew older, I became a *"diet expert"*, where I tried every magical plan to shape my body into society's ideal image. My weight fluctuated incessantly, and my self-esteem was hostage to my external appearance. I always felt in battle with my body. After my divorce, one of the greatest fears I had was to allow myself to have intimacy again. My body had transformed over the years, influenced by two births, my age, and the experiences that life had brought me. I had no idea how to make peace with these changes, so I resigned to the idea that intimacy was something that would only live in my past.

One particular memory stands out from a trip to Los Angeles where I went to film a program with my friend Neeta Bhushan. After filming, we had some time alone, and I confessed my fear of being intimate with a man again because my body wasn't the same as it was when I was 20. Neeta gave me a safe space to share thoughts that I never voiced before. She suggested we visit a Spa for a massage. The idea sounded incredible and I was grateful for the pampering.

We arrived at a Thai Spa in downtown Los Angeles in a five-story building. At the reception area, they gave us a set of clothes to change into. The clothes were the same for all the visitors, and that immediately made me feel more comfortable because I could blend in with the crowd without feeling the attention on me. I had an amazing massage, and then we moved on to the third floor which was for women only. Neeta explained to me that we were heading to the pools and steam rooms.

As soon as we entered that floor, we were asked to go into a dressing room and take off all our clothes. My body froze momentarily, and I felt extremely self-conscious. My mind started to race, voicing out all my fears in unison. *How can I get naked in front of all these strangers?! I'm overweight, and my body isn't perfect. Everything in my body has suffered the effects of age and gravity throughout the years, and I just can't take my clothes off!* Neeta put her hand on my shoulder to calm me down and invited me to look around.

And then, it struck me. Not a single person in that room had a *perfect body.* They were all-powerful, beautiful women of different age ranges, body types, and cultures who were simply sharing the space. I saw grandmothers with their granddaughters, I saw women who had had a mastectomy, I saw women with cellulite, and women who had sagging muscles. Others who were overweight, and others who struggled with their extreme thinness. None of that mattered in this space. They were all simply allowing themselves to BE. No labels, no clothes, no masks, no titles. It was just a gathering of women, existing together. Everyone was so different. Each of them was so beautiful in their natural way.

That was one of the most vulnerable moments of my existence, but also one of the most powerful lessons I needed to move forward. I decided that I was no longer going to let my body shape dictate how I presented myself to the world or how I felt about myself. I did not need to achieve any external standard of *perfection* to be allowed to enjoy my life, as true perfection emanated from the energy born *within me.*

When I started genuinely listening to my body, my relationship with food changed. Food became a source of energy and nourishment rather than something I had to avoid based on calories, or something I turned to when I needed to drown my emotions.

I started paying attention to what my body really needed. Became aware of how I felt before eating, during meals, and immediately after. This mindfulness allowed me to consciously choose what to feed my body based on the experiences I wanted to have in my life.

This also connected me to the energy of movement and how amazing I felt after working out. Exercise transformed from something I HAD to do to something I CHOSE to do.

I started following exercise routines that resonated with me; I even started dancing simply for the joy it brought me. My perception of myself underwent a radical change, and I learned to love and appreciate my body in every present moment.

Journal Insight Questions

The practice I'm going to share with you is called **Body Talk**. It is a concept that was developed and introduced to me by my friend Ronan Diego De Oliveira. He explains that all bodies are unique and that, instead of trying to force them to fit into molds they are not made for, we should learn to communicate with our bodies and foster a relationship with them. It helps us understand that our body, mind, and emotions all work together. What we think affects how we feel and vice versa.

Your mind, body, and emotions are in constant communication, giving each other important messages. Body Talk allows you to pay attention to those messages by becoming more aware. Start by connecting to your body right now.

Sit in a comfortable position and notice how you feel. Notice the sensations in your body. Start to focus on the tip of your head, then slowly scan your body all the way to your toes. What do you sense?

Then take your journal and reflect on the following questions:

- How does your body let you know that you are tired and need rest?
- What do you do when you feel tired? Do you push yourself or take a break?
- How do you feel when you are hungry? How does it feel when you are thirsty? Do you notice the difference?
- What does "comfort food" mean for you?
- What do you have when you want comfort food?
- When do you tend to look for "comfort food"?
- Is this related to your past stories? If so, what are those stories?
- What is your relationship to movement? What's the story you have about exercising?
- How often do you exercise?

- How do you feel before you begin exercising?
- How do you feel after exercising?
- When you look at yourself in the mirror now, do you love what you see?
- What would it take for you to love your body fully?
- What are you doing each day to love and nurture your body?
- What else can you do?

Practice constant body talk; notice your patterns of thought and how that affects your relationship with your body. One step at a time, one day at a time. The more you connect to your body and learn to fully love and accept yourself, the better you will feel, and the better care you will take of yourself.

This practice will connect you to your wings, which are just another way to name your inner power and your capacity to create an expansive life from a place of freedom.

"The meaning of life is to find your gift. The purpose of life is to give it away."

– Pablo Picasso

PART 6

Live Your Purpose: Strengthen Your Wings

When you acknowledge that you have a pair of beautiful wings on your back and that you are ready to fly the moment you decide to recognize them, then you will remember that it is your duty in this life to actively search for your feathers and strengthen your wings.

Living your purpose is all about taking action.
Consistent, imperfect, and brave action
that brings you closer and closer to where you
want to be. One small step at a time.

It is all about focusing on the impact that you want to create in the world. The legacy that you want to leave on this planet, and the reason why your soul decided to come to Earth.

This is about getting out of your head, leaving
your ego outside of the equation,
and allowing yourself to live your life to your fullest potential.

"The most valuable thing you can make is a mistake. You can't learn anything from being perfect."

– Adam Osbourne

CHAPTER 23

LET GO OF PERFECTIONISM

"*Perfectionism*," the dreaded word that creates an unnecessary weight on your shoulders, preventing you from truly doing what you love. *Perfection* is just a label that you create. An impossible measurement of success that will stop you from doing what you are meant to do on this planet. This is just an expression of a part of yourself that feels like it is *not good enough,* and therefore always seeks to give something more. Trying to achieve the impossible task of perfection is a desperate cry for attention, to feel that what you do is important and that you are *worth it.*

I have seen so many amazing people stop themselves from sharing their gift with the world because they feel is *not perfect. They* are not perfect. But in the same way that you create the label and stick it on your forehead, you can also change it to a label that is more empowering for yourself, like *excellence.* This doesn't mean that you should do mediocre things; it just means that you should aim for perfection, but be okay with excellence. It means you should bring the same compassion to yourself that you freely give to everyone else.

Take the first step toward your dreams, and then adjust along the way, without the extra added pressure of trying to DO something perfect or trying to BE perfect. I firmly believe that the world needs all human beings who are willing to help others use their voice and share their message because this is the only way we can truly change the current state of our Earth. So invite the *inner perfectionist* out of your reality, and invite freedom and creativity to direct your creation.

I spent many of my waking hours working with people around the world to help them learn to be kinder to themselves. I witnessed the unleashing of their inner power. I worked to empower them to let go of their limiting beliefs so they could be free to create from a place of expansion. In my coaching sessions, I helped many of my clients over-come their fear of perfection and trust themselves—to take the first steps toward what they wanted to create and then continue from there. I was very insistent that they didn't have to wait to have everything figured out to perfection before sharing their gift.

I was great at helping others do this for themselves, but I wasn't doing it for myself.

For years, I had worked comfortably behind the scenes of other people's dreams, not only because I truly love helping others, but also because a part of me was still waiting for everything to be *perfect* in my life before I allowed myself to pursue my own.

I had been wanting to write a book for years, but I wasn't a writer, so I told myself that I needed to prepare a lot more before I could share my words. I had always loved speaking on stage, but I didn't consider myself an expert speaker, so I let the idea sit on the back burner of my heart, waiting to hone my presentation skills before taking the stage. My list of dreams was neatly tucked away in a *things-I-would-eventually-do* drawer, but I never had the courage to start.

One day, after finishing a group coaching session with 300 amazing humans from all over the globe, I brought up the subject of being bold with your dreams. It was a beautiful session with many people getting out of their comfort zones and sharing their big goals with all of the community as we celebrated their courage for taking their first step. My daughter was sitting next to me in this session. Her face was serious as she read behind the mask of *the expert coach* I was wearing, and then called me out on my own fears.

"Mom, maybe you should apply some of the advice you give your clients to yourself," she said.

"What do you mean, honey?" I responded,

"You ask everyone to let go of their own bullshit and get into action, but you never do that for yourself. That's not okay, Mom."

Her words hit home.

I couldn't preach self-love and self-confidence to others if I didn't practice it myself. I couldn't tell others to act if I wasn't doing it. I wanted to explain to my daughter how difficult it was to start something so big, but then I realized that even at her young age, she had already done more to live her purpose in 20 years than what I had given myself permission to do in 45.

Avi had graduated as a shaman and a coach and was a living example of what you do when you have a clear purpose and are completely committed to your mission:

- She started a podcast with her best friend with zero experience.
- She learned to create some of the most beautiful reels and built a presence on social media.
- She started leading workshops and retreats every weekend.
- She created her website and her brand.
- She created and shared her photography portfolio with the world.

My daughter is half my age and had much fewer years of experience than me, yet she never let perfectionism or fear stop her from showing up fully. The only difference between Avi and me is that she *took action*. Fearless, bold and imperfect action that propelled her purpose.

When I see how she fearlessly shows up, pride and inspiration fill my heart, so I thought more deeply about my story around *perfection*. I always wanted to exceed everyone's expectations because a part of me was afraid to fail. My ego always wanted to shine as the *go-to global solver of problems,* but this was born from a place of not feeling good enough and the fear of abandonment if I didn't give things my 100%. But when I look back at my life to think about the greatest things I have achieved, they didn't have to do with perfection, but rather with doing things with excellence, fueled by passion.

I took a closer look on my life's experiences to find more moments were I had allowed myself to take bold actions without being 100% ready, and found so many moments of courage that reminded me that is was possible for me. That's how I started as a learning experience designer. With zero experience but a hunger to learn that led me to create beautiful online programs that have impacted thousands of lives. This is how I learned to be a leader, taking just one step at a time to become a guide for my team, and this is how I became a coach as well, by connecting from the heart and slowly getting better at my craft of helping others, one person at a time.

I now remind myself to let things flow instead of questioning every step and trying to control the results. Flow with what is presented in the moment. Flow with what my heart wants to do, and know that nothing has to be perfect before being born into the world. All I need to do is get started and then adapt to whatever comes along the way. This lesson extends beyond coaching. It applies to every part of my life. Every part of me that I want to improve, every part of me that is working to achieve what I want. That's when I give myself permission to let go of perfectionism and the false illusion of control. I just have to show up and take action! This reminded me of my experience with ballet.

I started dancing ballet when I was about 10 years old. At that time, I had neither the body nor the grace of a dancer. I remember trying to be like the other dancers in my class, but I was so far from where they were that I gave up after four months. I just believed *I wasn't cut out for it*. At 30, I decided to try ballet again. I still didn't match the ballerina ideal, but it didn't matter so much, because I really wanted to learn. Little by little, I learned to soften my movements, to enjoy the practice, and I went to class every week for 10 years. Finally, I achieved my goal of dancing in pointe shoes. At that moment, I felt like I had just climbed Everest!

The experience taught me the power of consistency and small steps forward, regardless of the results at the moment. All efforts create a compound effect, and everything contributes. I realized that the way we grow is when we have to learn to face our own challenges. That every time I try to control everything and try to *fix the lives* of others, I am only robbing them of their inner power to do it for themselves. Releasing the weight of walking the path of others as well as your own is extremely liberating! The only thing you have to focus on is taking YOUR small steps forward.

Remember not to wait until you have everything resolved before acting. Embrace experimentation and the joy of walking the path because it is through these small experiences that you gain wisdom and grow. This, my frind, is the biggest propeller for your wings!

Journal Insight Questions and Action Steps

There is a cool concept that I learned called the Marginal Gains Theory developed by Sir Dave Brailsford. This theory says that you can improve anything in your life by making lots of small incremental changes over time instead of trying to achieve success or make one big change all at once. Brailsford introduced the concept of making tiny improvements in every aspect of cycling. He believed that if they improved each area by just 1%, it would lead to significant overall improvement when combined.

Making tiny improvements consistently, even if they seem insignificant at the time, can lead to significant long-term success. The idea is that by making lots of these small improvements, you can gradually get better and better. It's like adding up lots of little wins to create a big win in the end. This allows you to get out of your *perfectionism-paralysis* and get into action.

Think about one area of your life you want to improve or one big project you have in mind right now that you want to be successful in.

- What is your current status? Where are you right now?
- What is your desired outcome? The ideal result you want to get if everything goes according to your plan?
- What are some of the things you can implement right now that will help you become 1% better at what you want to achieve? List at least 10.
- Develop a plan to implement these action steps, as well as a way for you to track your progress.
- Celebrate each step forward!

Remember that the goal of this exercise is not perfection but *progress*. Embrace the process of continuous improvement, and trust that even the smallest changes can lead to significant results over time.

CHAPTER 24

FOCUS ON YOUR IMPACT

*W*hen you do something for yourself, a feeling of satisfaction arises within you. But when you do something for others, help them see parts of themselves they've never seen before, help them see their inner power and regain their spark, that feeling of wholeness explodes in every cell of your being and expands. This is what it feels like to focus on your impact every day. It is an explosion of gratitude and fulfillment that words can't describe. You have to feel it.

It's about the legacy you want to leave on this planet. That is, if tomorrow you cease to exist, there will be something important that you are leaving behind, beyond material possessions. And legacy doesn't only mean solving the world's climate change problem or feeding the hungry. Your legacy is about how you want to be remembered. It's about sharing your gifts and your story with the world. It is about doing the small things in a BIG way because you never know who you are going to impact or who needs to hear something that only YOU can say.

After practicing coaching for many years, I understood the profound power of witnessing the transformation of another human being. After many conversations with my clients over the years, I realized that most people on this planet have never truly felt heard or seen. I also realized that this is a common thread that unites us all as humans: the need to feel that we matter and that our existence means something. Knowing that we are *enough* and that our story is *important*.

While I loved deep one-on-one conversations with my clients, part of me was asking for a bigger impact. I wanted to work with more people. I knew that the need for transformation in the world was much greater than what I could offer in a single session. It was time to get out of my comfort zone, to get out of the stable position I had for so many years behind the curtains. I felt the need to help more people at the same time. I needed more people to know that they too could live the life they always wanted.

Then, as always happens when you're ready, opportunities knocked on my door. I was invited to share my story on stage at a story club called Candelilla, founded by the visionary Anastasia Mora. She understood the transformative power that comes when everyday people share a part of their life with others. I was extremely nervous and my body was shaking as I stood in front of 100 people to share my voice for the first time.

I had just 7 minutes on stage. Seven minutes to share a story that had shaken the way I viewed my entire life. I got on stage and grabbed the mic with my hands shaking. The first 30 seconds felt like an eternity. Then I just let go of trying too hard and relaxed into sharing from my heart. At the end of those 7 minutes, I received a standing ovation, and I could see the people in the audience crying as they clapped.

It is not that I was an astounding speaker, or that my story is unique in the world. What created the massive impact is that it was MY story, and I was able to genuinely share it with others. That experience changed something transcendental in me. Witnessing the profound effect our words can have on opening hearts inspired me to continue doing this with more people, so I started giving seminars on how to live an extraordinary life with my friend Carla Egurrola.

On the day of my first seminar, we had 150 people in the room, and as I was getting ready to go on stage, my whole body froze again. I was no longer surrounded by other storytellers with an audience expecting a newbie, like at the Candelilla Club. This time, I was the center of attention, with an audience expecting a professional. The weight of responsibility for delivering something valuable to so many people fell on me like a ton of bricks.

I began a breathing exercise, and my sister Fio tried to calm me with her healing energy, but at that moment, no crystal or chakra movement could combat my inner saboteur. There were only 15 minutes left to start and I had to do something to fix my *"Inner Netflix"* that was showing me different horror scenes at the same time of everything that could go wrong. I called my friend and amazing coach Jason Goldberg for help.

I said, "Jason, I'm about to start this seminar, and I'm freaking out! What do I do?"

"Get out of your ego," he said

This was a hard blow straight to my liver. I was expecting words of encouragement, not this! I was hoping he would tell me how wonderful I was, not tell me to *"Get out of my ego?"* WTF! But then he explained to me, "Fran, this isn't about you. Think about it. If you can make just one person feel one percent better for just 1 minute, the world wins! So get out of your head and do what your soul wants you to do."

WOW. That was powerful and very true.

We often spend too much time worrying about what others may think or say about us, and that stops us from giving ourselves fully. If we just focus on serving *one* person, *one* heart, just for *one* moment, then we can change any fear into hope.

With newfound energy and confidence, I took the stage. As people walked into the room, I felt an overwhelming sense of love and connection. There were so many human beings seeking to discover something new about themselves. However, my confidence wavered when a woman approached the stage and looked directly at me.

- "Can I tell you something?" she said
- "Of course! Anything," I happily responded.
- "I just want to let you know I don't believe in this BS around personal growth, but I was forced to come here because my boss paid for the ticket. I just wanted to say that," she stated.

I was dumbfounded, but with the seminar about to start, I didn't have time to think too much about her words. I decided to do my best to shake off those harsh words, and set all my intention on serving my audience from the heart.

The seminar lasted eight hours. We explored our way of perceiving the world, danced, and imagined a future full of possibilities. There were moments of laughter and moments of tears, as we moved energy that had been stagnant for a long time. After eight hours, I felt so energized by the audience that I didn't even feel the fatigue in my body. At the end of the seminar, attendees lined up to express their gratitude. We hugged and took photos, and I listened to their stories with a heart full of gratitude.

Then I saw her again. The woman who had approached me at the beginning of the seminar was now in the line of people. Her face was red, and her eyes were swollen from crying. She was looking directly at me again. I felt a mix of trepidation and anticipation. I was ready to offer support, but I wasn't sure I could take another harsh comment after eight hours of pouring my heart and soul into the seminar! Finally, the woman came to me and asked permission to hug me.

When I opened my arms, and we hugged, she simply said, *"Thank you for giving me permission to dream. I had forgotten how to do that."* I allowed myself to cry with her for the next 20 minutes before she had to go back home.

That woman changed everything for me. SHE had been the reason I got up on that stage that day. Not only for all the people who went to the seminar but especially for HER. This was what Jason had meant. That's how impact truly feels like. That permission to dream is something that we all have access to. Knowing that we are powerful magical beings that are meant to live a beautiful life is something that has become my entire life's mission. This is why I wake up every day. This is the reason behind everything I do, to remind people just like you that you can FLY.

Journal Insight Questions

Here are some questions that will help you find the legacy that you want to leave in the world. This vision of your legacy will guide you on the impact that you create every day.

- If you had unlimited resources, what is the way that you would like to give back to the world?
- If you could solve any problem for the world, what would that be?
- What are the things that you do that align with your purpose and ignite you? What is your burning desire when it comes to creating an impact?
- What is your preferred way to share your gifts and talents with others?
- What is the one thing that you would like to be remembered for when you leave this Earth plane?
- What has been stopping you so far from creating your impact?
- What are you going to do to overcome any future challenge that comes your way from creating an impact?
- Who do you have to BE to create the impact that you want to create? What do you need to believe about yourself? How do you need to upgrade your mindset? What other lifestyle factors do you have to upgrade?

"You never lose by loving. You always lose by holding back."

– Barbara De Angelis

CHAPTER 25

ALLOW YOURSELF TO LOVE AND BE LOVED

*O*pening yourself up to love sounds beautiful. But when you've been hurt in the past, it may feel like one of the scariest things to do. Because when you open yourself to love and be loved, you have to take away the layers of protection to allow someone in. Then, and only then will you be able to experience a deep sense of connection.

Our brain is designed to protect us from danger, so it stores past experiences as memories, and it creates patterns that help us make sense of the world. These patterns also help our brains identify *signs of danger* when they are associated with events that make us feel hurt or betrayed, even when the new situation presenting itself is not dangerous at all. We also tend to look for patterns that feel familiar because our brain likes predictability, even if they serve us or not. This explains why even after we experience a horrible relationship, we may end up with a different person who may take us through the same situation.

So of course, it's scary to put yourself out there! No one wants to get hurt. The thing is, there is a way to break the pattern and create beautiful love relationships, and it all starts with *you*. With first falling in love with

149

yourself first, getting to know who you really are, what you like and don't like, what you need and what you want. Make sure you can heal and provide anything you need for yourself so you never depend on another person to *fill your tank*.

Then you follow this with awareness. Awareness of the beliefs and the patterns that you have around relationships, and how they guide your choices, so then you can release what doesn't serve you, heal what you need to heal, and then you can be ready to share your life with a partner.

The power of love will lift you in a way that no other energy can. The power of loving someone and allowing them to love you is a catalyst that will change you on a cellular level and bring the wind that will lift you off the ground so you can fly. This is the story of how I finally allowed myself to love again.

It was easy for me to talk about love to everyone while I safely guarded my heart against hurt, but with all the personal work I had done, I felt ready to welcome love back into my life. After my divorce, part of me felt like I had had my *quota* of romantic relationships for this lifetime, but another part of me craved a connection with a partner.

However, this time I would approach the topic of romantic relationships from a different perspective. I was no longer looking for my *other half* or the usual 50%-50% approach. Instead, the relationship I was looking for was made up of two whole beings who wanted to make the conscious decision to connect our lives in a strong partnership to co-create together. I wanted to feel loved, heard, and seen. I wanted to love fully without having to hide who I am, without masks, without holding back. And I wanted to create a space for my partner to do the same.

For a long time in my life, I had seen relationships from the lens of my own beliefs that didn't serve me. At first, I was looking for the *White Knight in Shining Armor* to come and take care of me. Back then, I saw my relationships as a burden, where I had to completely let go of myself to please the person I was with. Although these beliefs slowly faded, some of them were still alive in me.

I experimented with online dating but quickly realized it didn't fit what I really wanted. After my second date that came from an app, where I had to explain to a polyamorous bisexual man that I was a monogamous heterosexual, I just deleted the app. Then, my friend Cinthya introduced me to her friend Mauricio. She had told me about him many times before I met him, and I finally relented to allow myself to explore.

Mauricio and I connected very quickly. We met at a party and talked all night as if the rest of the world had disappeared. He was easy to talk with as if we had known each other forever. Before I knew it, the night was over and I went home. The next day, my friend Cinthya called me early in the morning.

"What did you think of him? He's perfect for you, isn't he?" she said.

I liked being around him. He made me feel comfortable in my own skin, but the part of me that was afraid of getting hurt immediately put up walls to protect my heart.

"Yes, but only as a friend," I replied.
"But he's perfect for you!" She insisted.
"I just want a friendship," I repeated.

It had been years since my divorce and I wanted a relationship, but I was very scared. I was afraid of getting hurt, of losing my freedom, of losing ME again and starting over. Despite my fear, Mauricio and I became very close friends. I could talk to him about everything and not hide any part of myself. I told him my story and my beliefs that past relationships had ingrained in me. I told him about my fear of getting too close to someone and my need to run away when this happened. He took note.

A year passed and our friendship became closer. He felt like home, and I felt comfortable with him. He patiently gave me my space to overcome my internal entanglements so we could be together. I invited Mauricio to come to one of my seminars. That day, he was the first person to arrive, and his special energy brought me a lot of peace. He was also the first person to hug me after the long day of the event.

After the seminar ended, we went to a friend's house to celebrate and started getting physically closer. Although I felt a mixture of excitement and exhaustion, his hug was too comforting. For the first time in a long time, I didn't want to run away. As I melted into his strong arms, something inside me changed. My fear of intimacy and being hurt began to fade, and I just wanted him to hold me. His presence silenced my self-sabotaging thoughts and allowed my heart to lead the way.

When it was time to say goodbye at the end of the night, Mauricio walked me to my car and got close to my face. Panic gripped me and I tensed, preparing to escape. Knowing me as deeply as he knew me, he didn't try anything bold. And as if he were approaching a baby deer, he simply gave me a soft kiss on the corner of my mouth and walked away.

I turned on my car and started driving home feeling dazed. Part of me was calm because he hadn't tried to kiss me, but another part of me was very confused. *What does a kiss on the corner of my mouth mean?*

I couldn't sleep or think clearly for the next two days. I waited for him to call me or stop by my house to explain what had happened. But he never called or showed up. I went from confusion to anger. There were so many conflicting signals! By the third day, I was exhausted by my internal battle. I got into my car, called him, and announced that I was coming to his place. My inner warrior appeared at his door and my thoughts screamed at him: *"I'm here, in front of you, now explain to me what that kiss on the corner of my mouth meant. NOW!"*

But all I could get out of my mouth was simply, "Hello."

He offered me coffee and a conversation, but what I really wanted was clarity and action. We talked for two full hours, while I waited patiently for him to make the first move.

But my patience was stretched thin, and I needed to know where I stood, so when he offered me more coffee, I stood up, grabbed his face with my hands, and planted a kiss on his face—a REAL kiss directly on the mouth.

After months of dating, I asked him what happened that day. Laughing out loud, he confessed that knowing that I had *escapism syndrome,* he had to allow me to get close to him and not the other way around so as not to scare me off. That was the beginning of our love story that lasted five years.

Although we parted ways as a couple, we remain good friends, and that relationship helped me heal my fear of intimacy and opening up to another human. Something I will be forever grateful, as it has allowed me to extend my wings like never before.

Journal Insight Questions

Before you can open your heart up to another person, you have to work on the most important relationship of your life, which is YOU. Once you love yourself completely and unapologetically, then you have to get clear on what you are looking for in a partner.

So take your journal and reflect on the following questions:

- What are you looking for in a relationship? What does a healthy and fulfilling relationship look and feel like for you?
- What are the five things that you love most about yourself?
- How do you like to receive love? - You can take the free quiz on the 5 Love Languages here: https://5lovelanguages.com/quizzes/love-language
- What are the things that make you feel loved and appreciated?
- What are the non-negotiables in your life?
- How do you manage conflict and disagreements with others?
- What is your preferred way to communicate in a relationship?
- How do you want to approach intimacy and vulnerability?
- What patterns do you notice from your past relationships that you don't want to repeat?
- What are some of the greatest lessons you've learned from past relationships?

"Your mind will always believe everything you tell it. Feed it hope. Feed it truth. Feed it with love."

– Leonardo Da Vinci

CHAPTER 26

CONNECT TO
THE ENERGY
OF EXPANSION

The energy you connect to will dictate what you can create in your life because where you bring your focus is what tends to grow. Notice how you feel with your thoughts, with the actions that you are taking every day, and with the people you are surrounding yourself with, that will tell you what you are attuning to.

When you do something that is not aligned with your soul, you will feel contracted. This is your body's way of letting you know that something is *not* for you. But when you do something that is aligned with your Higher Self, your heart will make you feel *expansive* in every corner of your body. This is the signal from the Universe for you to go deeper into doing what you are meant to be doing on this planet. This is your *purpose*.

The Universe works as a *spiritual investment system*, where the more you give, the more you receive in return. That's how abundance works. My friend Renata de Melo, a powerful healer and coach, has this phrase that she uses to invite more energy into your being that I love: *"Yes, more, please."* Use it as your personal mantra to attract more of what you want for your life, and if there is still a part of you that doubts about your gifts, or questions who you are before you go out there and serve the world with your gifts, get into *action*. The more you focus on helping others, the less you'll worry about your own fears.

I learned to attune to the energy of expansion during one of the most difficult moments in our recent history. When the COVID-19 pandemic put global normality on pause, I saw too many people fall into a pit of despair. This forceful earthquake shook the foundation of the structure that most of us had been accustomed to for years, and when something so fundamental changes, a common first reaction is fear of the unknown.

But I also saw the pandemic from a different angle. It seemed that the world needed to cleanse itself of old customs that no longer served humanity. It was an opportunity for all of us to reinvent ourselves and create a new future on a global scale.

Although I could no longer hold live seminars, many people needed help, especially during those difficult times. So together with my team at Mindvalley, we opened our consciousness to receive guidance on how to help so many people at the same time. I had a privileged position as an educational experience designer at Mindvalley Coach, the coaching division of Mindvalley, and with the guidance of Ajit (the founder), we sought to identify the biggest challenges our students were facing.

Through media reports, we realized that hundreds of thousands of people had lost their jobs. Many of them had been maintaining stable careers for years, and from one day to the next, they had lost everything; and with it, the security of a stable position. We spoke to hundreds of people who felt lost, unsure about their next steps, and filled with fear from the uncertainty. They believed that their college degrees and experience tied them to a single line of work, and as that disappeared, their identity disappeared with it.

People were confused about their future, feared for their families, and were isolated from each other, feeling trapped in their own realities. That's when we decided to create a space to offer hope and a new direction for their lives and careers. A path based on their own life experiences that could bring them new meaning while creating an impact in a world that desperately needed light.

Mindvalley Certifications were born.

Our mission as a company has always been to impact a billion lives. To achieve this, we needed the help of all the lightworkers in the world. We opened our first group of students in November 2020 to help people become certified as Business Coaches and Consultants. We received 160 humans who were ready to transform fear into hope and be able to begin redesigning the business environment on a global level.

This space was filled with many bittersweet moments. We heard stories of people who had lost everything and others who finally felt like they were truly alive. We worked with people of all ages who had a deep desire to uplift humanity, but who had become trapped in corporate labyrinths, unable to hear their inner calling. For four months, we connected with people from diverse backgrounds, cultures, religions, beliefs, ethnicities, and age groups.

We began as a diverse group united by a shared longing for hope and ended the journey as one large family of intertwined souls, and what started as an idea became a global movement: Our certified coaches are now agents of change themselves, creating impact and expansion for others around the world.

I realized that the energy of growth doesn't just come from having a mission. It comes from creating a movement that extends beyond your limits. That is the energy that I wanted to continue creating for my life and for the lives of the people I want to help transform. I realized that by preparing myself to fly, I am also helping everyone that I work with connect to their capacity to soar.

Action Steps

This somatic exercise will allow you to connect to your body so you can gauge what thoughts, situations, or people in your life feel contractive, which feels expansive. It will allow you to choose more consciously where you want to focus your energy and attention.

Close your eyes, take a few deep breaths, and:

- Recall a thought, situation, or person that makes you feel contracted. Where do you feel that in your body? How does it feel to you? What other emotions arise?
- Then recall a thought, situation, or person that makes you feel expansive. Where do you feel that in your body? How does it feel to you? What other emotions arise?

"It's already yours."

– The Universe

PART 7

MANIFEST YOUR IDEAL LIFE AND FLY!

Everything that you have been working on throughout your life is so you can create the life of your dreams. An ideal vision of what you want for yourself and those you love.

But before you can design your ideal life, you have to be clear about what you want to create. Having a vision of where you want to go helps you focus your energy on creating it.

When you think about your future, you have to
incorporate all aspects of who you are,
from the experiences you want to have, to the
people you want to share your life with,
to the impact that you want to create in the
world. This is when you get to FLY.

Flying is about dancing in a synchronous flow with the Universe.
It is what happens when you are completely aligned with your
soul's purpose, and everything you do is filled with a passion that
comes from the depths of your soul, all guided by intention.

This is when you wake up feeling energized knowing
that your mission is important. Remembering that you
are an indispensable piece in the wheel of life
and that you play a key role in the elevation of humanity.

CHAPTER 27

DESIGN YOUR
NEW REALITY

*I*n this chapter, you are invited to take your first *test flight* with your new wings. This is all going to be about manifesting your ideal vision and then creating a plan for you to be able to achieve it. I will invite you to dream without limitations and clearly visualize your future.

The first important thing to understand before you start is that the Universe is not a limited *pie,* that in order for you to have something, it means someone else gets less. This could not be farther from the truth! The Universe is not only abundant; it is *unlimited* and is always conspiring to give you everything you want. However, the challenge often lies in the fact that some of us simply don't know how to ask, or we don't believe that abundance is available to us.

We live in an era where anyone can manifest their dreams and become the best version of themselves if they choose to. And pay attention to the word "**CHOOSE.**"

I have seen people born into privilege who squandered their opportunities and others raised in poverty who led extraordinary lives. Ultimately, it all comes down to choosing what you want your life to be and then taking consistent action to create it. Here are some extraordinary examples of people who prove this to be true:

Oprah Winfrey—Born into poverty, began her career while still in high school working in radio. Today, she's a renowned talk show host, writer, campaigner, and Golden Globe winner. She built her life by aligning her work with her passion.

In her Golden Globes speech, Oprah remarked, "The single greatest wisdom I think I've ever received is that the key to fulfillment, success, happiness, and contentment in life is when you align your personality with what your soul actually came to do. I believe everyone has a soul and their own personal spiritual energy. When you use your personality to serve whatever that thing is, you can't help but be successful."

Ralph Lauren—Graduated from a high school in the Bronx, dropped out of college, and joined the US Army. He began his career as a sales assistant for Brooks Brothers, where his passion for design ignited. He firmly believes that we can create beauty from nothing.

Steve Jobs and Steve Wozniak—Embarked on their dream of developing consumer computer devices in Jobs' parents' garage after dropping out of college. Jobs started working at the age of 13 but never allowed challenging circumstances to dictate his future and always kept faith moving forward with perseverance.

You can start with just an idea, feed it with passion and consistency, and thus create anything you set your mind to. This is what fascinates me about coaching: It is not based on your past; it focuses on what you want to create in your future, and once you start seeing the Universe as an infinite play store where you can explore anything you want without limits, life becomes a game.

This is the story about how I learned to work with the Universe to build my Wings. I had been working on my vision for many years, refining it along the years of my journey, slowly learning to trust more in the process, and learning how to receive the many gifts that life had in store for me. I learned that every time I gave more, I always received more, and this constant dance of energies made me feel expansive.

I knew in my heart that I wanted to continue working with large groups of people. Diverse humans from all over the globe who had forgotten their inner power. I had given seminars and led many coaching groups, and I also wanted to speak on stage. The energy you can give and receive when you are on stage is a kind of electric buzz that you feel in every single cell. Speaking to a room full of wonderful souls has a tremendous effect on all the people who share the space.

My friends Neeta Bhushan and Sahara Rose invited me to host their Highest Self Weekend event in Austin in the summer of 2023. I didn't know exactly how to run a room, but my friend Neeta reminded me to connect to my heart and let it lead the way. It was a beautiful experience in a room with 350 women who were looking to connect to their highest selves and remember to love who they ARE.

As we connected during the event, there was one woman who approached me. She was in her mid-forties just like me, and she had to gather all her courage to come out of her shell of shyness. She told me that for the longest time in her life, she had felt isolated, and she had never believed she was important. She had always dreamed of sharing her message with others, but she just couldn't find the courage. Dismissing her worth.

She thanked me for being *"real"* on stage, telling me that it was the first time in her life that she got to see someone who didn't have the *"perfect body figure"* and talk with an accent on stage, and yet she saw me so full of confidence.

I thought deeply about that conversation. I didn't feel like the most confident person in the world, but I didn't allow that to stop me from living my purpose. I always thought that the fact that I shared my voice even when I felt nervous was insignificant—until that day. Until I was able to see the impact of my being OK with not having everything under control and still showing up. Of what that small act of courage did for myself was capable of doing for other humans.

When we returned inside the room and everyone got back in their seats, I locked eyes with the woman. I had the next segment of the event planned in my head, but at that moment, I realized there was something more important. So I got off the stage, walked between the attendees, and extended my arm to invite the woman on stage.

She was shaking hard. I could see in her eyes how nervous she was feeling. Every cell in her body screamed at her to stop, but her heart impulsed her to come with me on stage. I asked her to keep her gaze on me. When she stood in front of the big room, I asked her to share her story. She looked around the room and opened her mouth, but she couldn't speak. So I asked her to close her eyes and breathe. Telling her mind to step out for a moment so her heart could speak.

As I held her in my arms, she was able to grab the microphone and share her story. For the first time in her life, she was truly being heard with unconditional love. Once she finished her story, she opened her eyes and received a standing ovation applause. Her whole life changed after the moment that she finally said YES to herself.

These are the kinds of moments that I want more of. These are the kinds of transformations that I want to be able to witness. This is what abundance looks and feels like for me. A life where I get to share with amazing humans who remember why they came to this planet. Moments where I get to witness how others connect to their wings and fly again without fear.

Journal Insight Questions and Action Steps

The first step to creating a life of abundance is to be clear about what *abundance* means to you. Abundance, in my opinion, is not just about money. It encompasses all areas of your life: your health, your relationships, your experiences, your career, your character.

Everything that makes you **YOU**. Once you've crafted your big vision, it's essential to define how you want to feel. When you connect with the energy of abundance on a cellular level, you attune to attract that same energy into your life.

I discovered that manifestation is much easier than I ever imagined. All you have to do is be clear about what you want for your life, attune your energy to that, trust the process, and ask for guidance. From there, what follows is to take consistent action, one step at a time. Below are four things to consider:

Part 1. Get Clear on What You Want

Everything is created twice is a phrase often used by Stephen Covey, a consultant, public speaker, and author of "The 7 Habits of Highly Effective People." This means that before you can manifest something in the physical world, you must first have clarity of what that is that you want to create. Paint a clear vision in your mind.

I will use an example of why having clarity about what you want to create is KEY. Imagine going to a fancy restaurant. You are surrounded by beauty and everything is available to you because you are the most important client. The moment you walk into this restaurant, a happy person greets you at the door, you are given the best table in the restaurant, and your waiter comes with a huge menu of everything available to eat. All you have to do is CHOOSE, and your options are limitless.

You grab the menu and the waiter patiently waits for your order. However, you find the options overwhelming. You hesitate because there are too many options available, and you don't want to bother the waiter, so you simply say, "Bring me something hot." The waiter looks confused and starts pointing out all the hot dishes that are available to order. The kitchen staff is eager to serve you, but they need you to choose. The waiter gives you space to decide, knowing that it is ultimately your decision. You think a little more but remain undecided due to the number of options mixed with your complacent nature. You just say, "Anything hot will do, I'm okay with anything."

Then the waiter goes to the kitchen and brings you a hot dumpling that he found. When he hands you the plate, you see the little thing on your plate and feel disappointed. The ball of dough seems insignificant and you wanted something more, but you're not sure what. This is how the Universe works. We tend to think that somehow, it will know exactly what we want, and that when we see it, we will know what it was. But in reality, the Universe is just waiting for you to connect with what you want so it can show you the way to get it.

Write Your Life Vision

Imagine that you have unlimited resources. Time, money, health, love, friendships, support, everything, and anything you want and need to live an extraordinary life. Write it down as if your ideal life IS a reality three to five years from today.

- What does an extraordinary life look and feel like for you?
- What would you do with your time?
- How would you show up in the world?
- Who are you spending time with?

- How are your relationships?
- Where would you travel?
- How would you contribute to the world?

Part 2. Attune Your Energy

If you have ever listened to music, you will understand the concept of attuning.

Imagine that you open Spotify and you want to feel calm and inspired at that moment. Naturally, you would select a relaxing piano piece or something similar. But what happens if you choose a hard rock song? You will probably feel many things, but calmness and serenity will not be among them!

The same thing happens when you want to manifest something in your reality; it is essential to tune in to the energy of what you want to create. It may sound a little *"woo-woo,"* but it's based on science! Everything is made up of energy, and your thoughts and emotions have a direct impact on your physical reality.

Dr. Masaru Emoto's studies on water molecules illustrate this concept (you can read more about this study online). He demonstrates how the structure of water molecules changes depending on the energy they are exposed to.

Also, Dr. Bruce Lipton explains in his book *"The Biology of Belief"* how our beliefs can affect our biology and health. Lipton argues that our thoughts and beliefs can influence our cells and genes, impacting our overall well-being. He suggests that by changing our beliefs, we can positively affect our health and happiness.

Everything is connected and everything has the same origin of creation. To manifest effectively, you must match your energetic frequency with what you wish to create. **This is called the law of resonance:** You attract what you believe you are.

Raise your vibration to attract high-frequency relationships, situations, and abundance.

Daily practices, like gratitude, can help. Remember that what you focus on tends to expand. So focus on what you want to grow in your life. This serves as the fuel that powers your day. Day after day. And it is how you can create your reality on your own terms.

For you to be able to create your ideal life, what do you have to incorporate into your lifestyle, your mindset, and your being?

- What are the practices that make you feel elevated, excited, and expanded?
- How are you going to incorporate these practices into your everyday life?
- Who are the people that you want to surround yourself with? Why?
- What do you need to learn to raise your energy?
- What else can help you attune your energy to what you want to create?

Part 3. Trust the Process and Ask for Guidance

We have many ideas about how our lives *should be,* the opportunities we *should have,* and how the people around us *should act,* but life often unfolds differently from the plans we have carefully created in our minds.

This is perfectly OK. This is where the act of trusting the Universe to show us the way comes into play. Your plan may seem like the ideal path to follow, but there could be an easier, more satisfying path waiting to reveal itself.

Think of the Universe as your *Waze.* All you have to do is know your destination and allow it to guide the way. I ask the Universe to guide me explicitly so that I really understand (loudly and with neon signs) so I don't miss the messages I need to see. This is how I discovered the courses I needed to learn from, connected with amazing people at events, and received the best invitations, so I could live my purpose differently.

You are not alone. Remember that help is always available for you when you are ready to receive it; all you have to do is ask!

- What support do you need to create your ideal life?
- What teachers or mentors can help you along the way?
- How are you connecting to your intuition?
- What practices can help you connect to what your heart wants to say?

- How does it feel in your body when you know that something is meant for you?
- How does it feel in your body when you know that something is not meant for you?

Part 4. Take Consistent Action

And the final part of manifestation is to DO something about your dreams. You don't need perfection or monumental efforts to live your ideal life. The essential thing is to have constant progress.

Think of it like riding a bicycle. The first few strides may seem challenging, but once you're pedaling steadily, everything becomes easier. It is the forward movement that becomes one of the things that keeps your bike upright and in the right direction. Don't wait for circumstances to be perfect to act. Act first and course-correct along the way.

This is about taking one step at a time. About prioritizing your dream and giving it life through consistent action.

- What is your level of commitment toward creating your ideal life? (from 1-10)
- Why is this important for you?
- What will happen if you achieve what you want to create in your vision?
- What will happen if you don't achieve your vision?
- What has been stopping you from living your dream life?
- How will you overcome any challenge that shows up in the future?

CHAPTER 28

HONOR
YOUR LIFE

*W*e often focus so much on planning our future that we forget the valuable lessons our past can teach us. While having goals is important, if we only focus on what we want in the future, we may always feel like we are missing out on something. We will always be chasing *something* that we don't have yet. That's where honoring your past comes into play.

Your past is not just a bunch of old things that happened to you. It's the story of how you got to where you are today. It is a reminder of your strength, your successes, and even the difficult times you have been through. Your past made you who you are and makes you unique. This uniqueness is part of the superpower that only you can share with the rest of the world.

Dan Sullivan shares more about this idea in his book *The Gap and The Gain*.

- **The Gap** talks about the space between where you currently are versus where you want to be. This often leaves you feeling frustrated because you are always chasing your next goal.
- **The Gain** is the progress you have made from where you started. It is about recognizing and appreciating the growth and improvements you have made throughout your life journey. This approach can lead to greater satisfaction, gratitude, and motivation.

I used to feel like I was always *falling behind* in my goals, or that others were *way ahead* of me. Now, I choose to focus on a simpler question: ***"Am I better than last month, last year, or even yesterday?."*** This shift in focus keeps me grounded in my own progress and reminds me that every step forward is a personal victory.

When I reflected on my own life, I could clearly see all the challenging moments I have faced, such as getting pregnant at 19, my son's accident, times of fear and scarcity, heartbreaks, and times when life didn't go as planned. These situations were hard and painful, but they are what made me who I am today. They made me stronger, more resilient, kinder, more loving, and wiser, and they allowed me to enjoy everything that comes my way.

As I reviewed my life, I realized that my life was not just a collection of stories, but rather a road map that I knew somehow my soul had planned for me to be where I am today. I understand now that every important event was a way to find more feathers for my wings. Each of those great moments changed me, helped me expand, think differently, and explore different parts of my being. They also taught me to be lighter and not take everything so personally. And I needed that lightness to be able to fly.

Below are some of the many challenges I faced in my life, and these are also the things that helped create the person I am today.

My Son Eduardo's Birth at a Young Age

My son was born just four months after I turned 20. That was the moment I understood the meaning of true love. It was also the moment when I learned to be super organized with my time (so I could study, work, and be a mom).

Eduardo's Accident

I was 22 years old when I almost lost my son in an accident. I have never experienced so much fear and helplessness at the same time in my life, but I also see that it made me incredibly resilient and was the most powerful way for me to know with certainty that there is something bigger than us supporting our journey always. It connected me with spirituality, taught me to let go of the things I can't control, to trust that the Universe has my back, and paved the way for me to become a healer years later.

Eduardo's Autism Diagnosis and Multiple Therapies

Edu's autism diagnosis affected me greatly, but it also taught me that life doesn't always go according to "*plan*" and that that is still perfect. Going to therapy every week taught me how perseverance and consistent action can change any outcome, no matter how great. It also showed me the power of taking small steps forward, even when you have no idea what's coming next. In life, there are no impossible things, and we write the future with our daily choices.

My Marriage

Seventeen years with a person brings all kinds of lessons, and I know that everything happens for a reason. Those years taught me to truly commit, to face any difficult situation that comes my way, and to understand that everyone has a completely different way of seeing the world, and that's okay.

My Daughter Avi's Birth

My daughter was a wonderful ball of energy from the moment she was conceived. She taught me that life is too precious to be witnessed from the sidelines and that we have to enjoy every second just because. I also learned to have more fun, be able to laugh at myself, and stop my *inner perfectionist* from sabotaging my life.

My "Dance Mom" Years

Although there was a lot of running from one place to another, during rehearsals, makeup, costumes, and the stress of competitions, being the mother of a high-performing dancer taught me through my daughter's experience the importance of discipline, the power of camaraderie and the power of doing what needs to be done despite being afraid.

My Personal Honeymoon

The time I had to spend some time alone with myself taught me the joys of traveling light, putting mental baggage aside, and focusing on just being. It taught me to let go of the idea of trying to control everything, it reconnected me with my own needs and desires, and it taught me how to let go of guilt and live life fully. It also allowed me to go on adventures without planning too much and enjoy every experience as if it was my last.

My Divorce

The most important lesson from my divorce was the power of forgiveness in all situations. It taught me how to set healthy boundaries and to use my voice to communicate what my heart wanted. I also learned that it's okay to separate from a partner when you're both going down different paths. The fact that you are no longer in a relationship does not mean that there has to be any conflict between the parties.

My Coaching Career

My career as a coach opened the doors for me to explore the many facets of our human nature, connect with my purpose, do something I love every day, and remember that each person is responsible for the life they choose to create. It taught me to be a better listener and to leave any judgment out of my conversations.

Speaking on Stage

Giving seminars and being able to share my voice with large audiences is one of the most expansive experiences I have ever felt in my life. Being able to work in a room full of like-minded souls working together to create something magical in their lives has been one of the most exhilarating reminders of what a life full of purpose feels like.

My 5-year Love Relationship After my Divorce

Those 5 years with Mauricio were a beautiful journey to rebuild my ability to trust and connect deeply. I went from a place of fear of getting too close to another person to healing my fear of closeness.

My Inner Circle

My parents, brothers, and sisters are a reminder of what it feels like to have a close tribe that supports you. Not only do I fully trust them with my life, but I also know that we have each other's backs no matter what happens in life.

My close friends always make me feel at home and remind me that chosen families are real, and that is priceless.

Witnessing My Children Fly on Their Own

As I look at my children, my heart feels full seeing their incredible transformation. These once helpless babies who depended on me for their survival have grown into powerful adults. I realized that my role as a mom changed. It's no longer about fixing things for them but rather about witnessing their journey as they spread their own wings.

I have always believed that the most important thing I could do for my children was to teach them how to listen to their hearts and pursue what makes them genuinely happy, whatever experiences they choose.

Eduardo's life has been a testament to the power of perseverance and incorporating one's unique abilities. He went from a grim autism diagnosis as a child to pursuing his passions in fields like video game design, voice acting, and even graduating from culinary school.

His passion for superheroes, fueled by his Asperger syndrome, has given him an incredible ability to concentrate and retain information. It's very inspiring to see how he has turned what some might see as a cognitive difference into his unique superpower.

For years, we tried to ask the system to allow him to work. Open up an opportunity for him to do something productive that was satisfying for him. For years, we found doors closing one after another, but he never gave up. He now works in something he loves, and he's completely independent. Perseverance and love always kick the butt of closed minds!

My daughter became a shaman, healer, and coach. Her entrepreneurial spirit guided her to share her voice with the world and create spaces for others to also find their purpose. She is now part of a global movement of young entrepreneurs who are helping other young people start and grow heart-centered businesses, to help create a global impact in the way we approach life.

Being able to see that my two children are grown and doing what they love brings great joy and satisfaction to my life. Knowing that they are both pursuing their own dreams and passions and watching them live their individual lives allows my heart to feel at ease, knowing that no matter what happens in my life, they are ready to fly on their own.

I also understood that everything in my life has happened FOR me. Everything has been perfectly designed in PRO of my unique journey! Being able to map it all was a confirmation that the Universe supported me all along, and this gave me the strength to fly.

Journal Insight Questions

Take a moment to look back at your past and notice how far you have come; notice the times when you felt afraid of doing something but you went ahead and did it anyway. The times when you experienced a heartbreak that felt like the end of your world, and yet you came out stronger on the other side. Write the KEY moments that shaped who you are today.

Think about the moments that marked you. The moments that contributed to the person that you are today. Write them down, all of them. Then reflect on what each moment brought to you. How you learned and how you changed because of them. Then appreciate everything that has come your way.

Every win and every challenge. Notice how each one of those moments has taken you exactly where you needed to be. How each of those feathers has built a very important part of your wings and has given them power for you to remember your ability to FLY.

CHAPTER 29

BUILDING
THE NEXT
ITERATION
OF MYSELF

*M*y 40s brought me a new opportunity to think about the next version I want to design for myself. My wings are now fully grown, and I can feel how all the feathers collected from every experience I have had in my life contributed to making them stronger. It's time to fly!

I no longer worry about what others might think of me and instead focus more on what feels right. I learned to question the usual rules that were imposed on me as a child and to embrace the new rules that I chose for myself as an adult. I understood that everyone is responsible for creating their own reality, and it is not my responsibility to fix anyone. The only life that is truly my responsibility is my own, and this allows me to create from a place of unlimited freedom.

I learned to say NO and mean it. The complacent girl in me finally died, and now she made room for the empowered woman who can choose what and who she gives her energy to.

I let go of friends whom I no longer feel aligned with the life I want to lead, I released the need to put myself in uncomfortable situations, and I simplified the complexity of my daily tasks.

I only invite people who make me feel expansive into my life. I incorporated more joy into my daily routines, I made room for movement and fun in my routine, I allowed myself to take breaks when I need them, and I released the lump in my throat that didn't allow me to share my truth. And, above all, I understood that my greatest and most important role on this planet is to simply BE.

To live each day as if it were the first and the last, not take everything so seriously, and allow myself to enjoy the journey that each moment brings, focusing on all the feathers that exist around me, waiting to be discovered and added to my powerful wings.

I am back in the playground of my childhood years, shedding the layers I had imposed on myself in adulthood, and rediscovering the magic of infinite possibilities. As I let go of the weight of my own self-imposed limitations, I feel lighter than I had ever felt before. Although I have made many changes over the years, I am ready to review the vision I want for my life in the next quarter of my existence on Earth.

As I sat by my butterfly garden and allowed my heart to connect with my soul's calling, this was the message that flowed through me. My life vision:

I live in Costa Rica, in a beautiful home full of natural light and high vibrational energy. The place where I live is surrounded by nature, there are many fruit trees, colorful flowers, and lush gardens. The background of my house is decorated by majestic mountains that provide me with daily inspiration.

I wake up to the sounds of birds and the smell of nature coming through my windows, and my mornings are always full of excitement for the day ahead. I have breakfast in front of my butterfly garden and witness life blooming in every corner of my property. It is my personal paradise, and I feel in a constant state of inspiration and gratitude.

I have a beautiful loving relationship with my partner, and we really enjoy spending time together. We have a deep connection based on love and mutual admiration. We set aside special moments every day to nurture our relationship and have deep, honest conversations.

We grow together as human beings, learning more about ourselves, and also our individual life experiences. We learn new skills and competencies that allow us to grow intellectually and emotionally all the time. All this contributes to increasing the vitality of our relationship.

We also travel to exotic places for two months each year, where we can discover new areas of the world and new aspects of our relationship. During these trips, we immerse ourselves in the local culture, eat delicious food, learn about different traditions, and connect with the people we meet.

My partner and I are in the best shape of our lives. We are lean, muscular, healthy, and vibrant. Life feels amazing on a cellular level, and we enjoy it to the fullest. We have incredible flexibility and mobility, and we feel more attracted to each other every day. We incorporate activities like yoga, dance classes, hiking, and outdoor adventures to maintain our physical and emotional vitality.

We have complete financial freedom, no debt, and more than enough money in our bank accounts to give us the freedom to choose how we want to experience life. My coaching business, my books, and my speaking engagements provide us with a very generous income. We also have several investments that will take care of our future so that we can retire peacefully and continue enjoying the life we want on our terms. Our investments not only secure our future but also allow us to contribute to philanthropic causes and make a positive impact on the world.

I am completely in love with the work I do because it gives me incredible satisfaction and creates a huge ripple effect in the world. I have published more than five books that have been successful in both English and Spanish and have been read in all countries of the world. My books inspire people from diverse cultures and backgrounds, fostering a sense of global unity.

I am an international speaker who teaches seminars around the world to help people find and embody their life purpose, and I am also invited to speak on different stages around the world. I have directly impacted over 100,000 human lives awakening to their inner power around the world. Through my speaking engagements, I empower people to unleash their potential and make positive changes in their lives and communities.

Thanks to my online programs, thousands of people have changed the direction of their lives and careers, going from working in environments that did not satisfy or meet their needs, to creating heart-centered businesses, aligned with their soul's purpose. That creates an impact in their lives and their communities around the world.

I feel incredibly fulfilled and grateful to have the opportunity to help so many people live the best version of themselves because this is aligned with my soul's purpose, which is to remind people of their inner power and the fact that everyone can live an extraordinary life.

I facilitate life-changing retreats in beautiful locations around the world, where I meet with groups of inspiring people to co-create change on our planet. These retreats create a global network of changemakers collaborating on meaningful projects for a better world.

I have an incredible team of 10 people who support my mission and handle all operational aspects of my business so I can focus on creating impact with fun and ease. My team members are also aligned on creating a massive impact in the world. Each of them can explore their zone of genius and grow with my company toward their own dreams.

I have a financial expert who handles all the company's money management, two customer service specialists who provide care to the people we impact, two marketing specialists who help me expand the impact of my company, two social media managers who manage the strategy and outreach of my message, one learning experience designer who creates the online educational part of the business, a manager who helps me handle all logistics and operations, and a live events manager who helps me organize the seminars and retreats.

My team shares my vision and values, which makes our work not only productive but also enjoyable for everyone. We truly love and care for each other as a family.

Life is easy, fun, and full of joy, and purpose. Every day when I open my eyes, my heart is filled with gratitude for my extraordinary life.

The message that flowed through me was meant for myself, so why do I share it?

The answer is that the wonderful life I live, as described in the message, is available to you too. Certainly, the details will be different, but you can wake up excited every day, love fully, engage with your work, and live a life that perfectly aligns with exactly who you want to be, with who you were meant to be. All you have to do is choose to create this life that is available to you.

Unleash your wings and fly my friend!

ACKNOWLEDGMENTS

To my mom, Victoria: You have been the greatest pillar of my life. You have been by my side in every moment of my existence, and you have helped me carry the weight of my problems with a determined strength that I will never have enough words to thank you for. You taught me what the power of unconditional love and consistency can do for a human being, and I thank you not only for raising us with such strong conviction but also for your incredible constant presence in my life and that of my children.

To my dad, Antonio: Thank you for opening my consciousness to a whole new magical world of subtle energies, for helping me question my reality, and for encouraging me to always work for what I want to create without any fear in my heart. Thank you for teaching me to let go of what no longer serves me, to learn to see life more easily, and thank you for passing on your love for plants and books!

To my son, Edu: Thank you for giving me the gift of becoming a mom, and for allowing me to see that no matter how difficult things get, you can always overcome whatever comes your way if you really fight for it. Thank you for your noble heart and your unconditional love, and for never losing hope. I'm so proud of you!

To my daughter, Avi: Thank you for being a pillar in my life, for teaching me that doing what the heart calls is more important than doing it perfectly, and for having the courage to tell me things as they are when I needed it most. Thank you for being an inspiration of what courage and determination can create in your life and for being you. You make my heart sing with happiness and pride my love!

To my brother, Antonio: Thank you for always making me feel like I am the most important person in the world. From the time you studied abroad and sent me the most beautiful letters in the world to our weekly conversations that make me feel that I am capable of anything.

To my brother, Fede: Thank you for being my best friend growing up, for your constant protection and guidance in navigating life, and for the important reminder that life is supposed to be simple, and that makes it more fulfilling.

To my sister, Fio: Thank you for being my twin sister for so many lives. Thank you for existing! Thank you for so many lives together, for being my constant person in every moment of my life, for the long conversations, the endless hours of laughter, for your heart, and your energy. You are a breath of fresh air full of fairy dust!

To my sister, Estefa: Thank you for sustaining me through one of the most difficult times of my life and reminding me to believe that divine help is always available. Thank you for teaching me the strength to achieve what I want, no matter what life throws at me, and even for the Backgammon games that you never let me win.

To my brother, Jeanpi: Thank you for always being there for me, for protecting me, for your incredible advice, for helping me get through the scariest moments of my life with fierce determination, and for always being by my side.

To my friend, Cinthya: Thank you for being like another sister to me for all these years that we have walked through life together, for always calling me to see how I am, even when life is chaotic, for our endless conversations to fix the world, and for being my unconditional person.

To my friend, Neeta: Thank you for showing me the way out of fear, for helping me reconnect with the woman in me, for the many birthdays we shared, for the life experiences that you have gifted me that have allowed me to grow as a human, and for being my greatest support in being able to share my voice with the world.

To my friend, Ajit: You have no idea how grateful I am to you! Thank you for opening the doors to the world of coaching, for the unlimited opportunities, for helping me tame my overthinking mind, and for helping me simplify the most complicated situations. You have been a great role model!

This book would not have been possible without all of you. Thank you for being key in my life, and for all your love and support.

To many more years of amazing things to come!

I LOVE you.

ABOUT THE AUTHOR

Francesca Facio is a Human Optimization Coach, International speaker, and Consultant in life design.

She is a woman who knows the journey of personal reinvention very well. A Latin American woman raised in Costa Rica, she grew up guided by the rules of a society that imposed impossible standards on women. She raised two kids while juggling two jobs, running a home, and trying to fit into the "perfect woman" model for years.

After almost losing her son to a terrible accident, helping her son navigate autism, being near bankruptcy, and going through a divorce, she found a way to turn her life around and redesign it to create a new reality for herself and her family.

As a Master coach and head of Mindvalley Certifications, she has more than 12 years of experience in the realm of personal growth and has worked with over 2,000 people from all over the globe. She shares her personal story as well as her professional experience to inspire readers to redesign their lives on their own terms.

With a postgraduate degree in Happiness & Organizational well-being from the University of Nebrija, Spain, and a certification in Pranic healing, she combines the Western practices of Coaching with the Eastern practices of healing to help her clients find their life purpose, ignite their passion, and take the steps toward their personal freedom.

To learn more about the author, you can visit: franfaciocoach.com

Printed in Great Britain
by Amazon

44485302R00109